Party! Party! for CHILDREN'S MINISTRY

Plenty of Parties, Carnivals, and Special Events

by Susan L. Lingo

Group

Loveland, Colorado

DEDICATION

I will rejoice in the Lord, I will be joyful in God my Savior
(Habakkuk 3:18, NIV).

Party! Party! for Children's Ministry

Copyright © 1996 Susan L. Lingo

Credits

Book Acquisitions Editor: Mike Nappa
Editor: Lois Keffer
Chief Creative Officer: Joani Schultz
Copy Editor: Sandra Collier
Designer and Art Director: Jean Bruns
Cover Art Director: Liz Howe
Computer Graphic Artist: Randy Kady
Cover Illustrator: Greg Hargreaves
Illustrator: Sharon Holm
Production Manager: Ann Marie Gordon

Unless otherwise noted, Scriptures quoted from The Youth Bible, New Century Version, copyright © 1991 by Word Publishing, Dallas, Texas 75039. Used by permission.

Library of Congress Cataloging-in-Publication Data

Lingo, Susan L.
    Party! Party! for children's ministry : plenty of parties,
carnivals & special events / by Susan L. Lingo.
        p.   cm.
    Includes index.
    ISBN 1-55945-609-4
    1. Children's parties. 2. Christian education of children.
3. Church work with children. I. Title.
BV1475.2.L55 1996
259' .22—dc20   96-5876
                                                          CIP

10 9 8 7 6 5 4 3 2 1   05 04 03 02 01 00 99 98 97 96
Printed in the United States of America.

Table of Contents

Let's Party!

What's more fun and festive than a children's party or special celebration? Colorful, creative, and carefree, *Party! Party! for Children's Ministry: Plenty of Parties, Carnivals, and Special Events* focuses on fun and is designed to delight both party goers and hosts. Each party or carnival event supplies you with all the ideas you'll need from dazzling decorations to ready-to-run-off invitations and public announcements. Parties and carnivals include:

- Christmas in July?
- Hoppin' Easter Hoopla
- Summer Snowball Party
- Hula Hula-Baloo
- The Instant Party
- Jungle Jamboree
- The Great Cookie Carnival and many more!

So stir up a little party-mania, and have fun celebrating holidays or "any days"!

Party Celebrations

Introduction to Party Celebrations

Church leaders, teachers, and even parents may ask, "Why do we have parties for kids?" "Who wants to organize parties—they take so long!" and "Aren't parties just a frivolous waste of time?"

The truth is, kids need parties and special events. Kids need to know that church isn't just a place for serious lessons—it's also a place for serious fun. But parties for *learning?* Absolutely! Children's parties are often overlooked in our bid for serious "book" learning. But parties can be wonderful educational tools. What can parties and special get-togethers offer in the area of Christian education? Read on…

● **Acceptance.** Parties are happy, welcoming events. Even kids who are shy and withdrawn respond to the warmth created by fun, food, and friends. Parties help kids learn that they're welcome and accepted—without any pressure to "perform."

● **Fellowship.** Parties offer a great opportunity for friendships to develop. Everyone seems friendlier when worries about school, grades, and peer pressure are put aside. Kids who seldom speak to each other at school are often very open in an atmosphere of celebration. At parties, people smile and laugh…and it's catching! Because the relaxed atmosphere of a party is conducive to building friendships, it's great to plan parties as icebreakers at the beginning of the year.

● **Confidence.** Parties offer kids opportunities to try their wings in a variety of games, crafts, activities, and other special pastimes in a nonthreatening atmosphere. These kinds of celebrations can be real confidence-builders as kids learn that having a good time with friends is more important than "winning" or giving stellar performances.

● **Community building within your group.** Parties help kids bond in special ways. Building identity in a group and coming together for a common purpose—even a party—strengthens the ties of each individual to the group. Kids learn that they're part of a church family who shares fun times.

You can use parties as powerful, social teaching tools, as enrichment for lessons, and as just good, ol' fashioned fun! And you don't have to shudder with "preparation dread" if you keep parties simple and snappy. The basic components of any party are really quite simple: invitations, decorations, activities, food, party favors, and…kids! *Party! Party!* is designed to help you expertly plan, prepare, and carry off successful parties. All you add is kids!

HINTS FOR SUCCESSFUL PARTIES

Truly successful parties have four things in common: **upbeat environments, welcoming icebreakers, graceful closures, and memory-makers.** Use these hints and tips and you'll put on successful parties every time!

● **Party environment is crucial.** All the games, food, and fun activities you've planned may bomb if the mood and atmosphere aren't welcoming. Party environment revolves around physical decor and general atmosphere. Snappy decorations centered around a particular theme lend cohesion to parties and special events. Use bright colors and upbeat background music to set the stage for energetic, joyous themes. Soft lighting and lots of twinkling Christmas tree lights create a slightly calmer—though equally joyous—atmosphere. Decorations, lighting, and music give parties special pizzazz!

With each of the parties in this book you'll find suggestions for a simple-to-create party environment that is exciting and memorable. You may even wish to let your young guests help "deck the halls." All you have to do is set out colorful crepe paper, tape, and bouncy balloons, then watch your party take off!

Perhaps the most important part of creating a pleasing party environment is making guests feel welcome the moment they arrive. When you greet each guest by name with a cheerful smile and a quick pat on the shoulder, kids will know they're genuinely welcome.

● **Don't neglect icebreakers.** No one enjoys walking into a group of people—even a group of friends—and feeling out of place. Put kids at ease the moment they arrive by kicking off every party with an icebreaker that introduces kids to each other and draws them immediately into the happy celebration. Icebreakers may include fun activities such as scavenger hunts for different names, partner puzzles, and find-a-friend interviews. Each party in this book includes exciting (and often zany!) icebreakers to welcome kids and get them immediately involved.

● **Party closure puts an exclamation point on the good time you've had together.** Closure brings a graceful end to your special event and allows kids to leave in the happy glow of fellowship and fun. A good closing will summarize your party theme, give kids something to take home, and include a verbal expression of your delight in the time you've spent together. Remember, the point of your party is to have kids leave with smiles on their faces—and in their hearts!

● **Make your parties memorable occasions.** Simple touches included in your party preparations can create memorable events for you and your guests. Consider tacking up a string of colorful Christmas tree lights for a party in the spring. Or plan your party at a surprising time or place, such as on a summer evening at a school playground. Include plans for memorable party favors kids can create during your special event. Kids might decorate rocks for perky paperweights or create candles-in-a-can to "light up" their dinner tables and their memories. And don't forget plenty of film and an instant-print camera to capture party memories as they happen. Decorate funny poster-board frames, and let kids take their photos home from the party to share with their families and friends. And remember, special hugs and smiles are the best "party favors" of all! Warm memories of great together times last long after photos have faded and favors are forgotten.

GETTING STARTED

Great parties don't just happen—they're made! All it takes is organization, creativity, and a little elbow grease. With all of the parties in the following pages you'll find creative games, craft activities, food ideas, suggestions for decorations and invitations, and unique tips to make your special events memorable. Feel free to mix and match ideas and adapt activities so they'll work well with your kids.

Getting organized for your parties couldn't be easier! Simply use the Shopping List found at the end of each party suggestion. Or photocopy the reproducible Party Planning Guide, Smart Shopper's Checklist, Party Countdown! checklist, and the Games & Activities List. Fill in the forms, and your party is planned! You may want to keep your lists in a handy "party portfolio" folder so you'll always have them ready in a snap! Use self-stick notes to mark the pages of the party you've chosen so you can quickly refer to the games, activities, food, decorations, and invitations you'll be using. Armed with party page numbers and handy checklists, you're ready to begin!

PARTY PLANNING GUIDE

Theme: _____ (p._____)

Date: _____

Place: _____

_____

From: _____o'clock **To:** _____o'clock

Number of kids expected: _____

Helpers: _____ (phone) _____

_____ (phone) _____

_____ (phone) _____

Guest list:

_____ (phone) _____ (reply) _____

_____ (phone) _____ (reply) _____

_____ (phone) _____ (reply) _____

_____ (phone) _____ (reply) _____

_____ (phone) _____ (reply) _____

_____ (phone) _____ (reply) _____

_____ (phone) _____ (reply) _____

_____ (phone) _____ (reply) _____

_____ (phone) _____ (reply) _____

_____ (phone) _____ (reply) _____

_____ (phone) _____ (reply) _____

Special Notes:

SMART SHOPPER'S
CHECKLIST

Invitations
- ☐ Envelopes
- ☐ Stamps
- ☐ _____
- ☐ _____

Decorations
- ☐ Crepe paper
- ☐ Balloons
- ☐ Poster board
- ☐ Markers
- ☐ Construction paper
- ☐ Tissue paper
- ☐ _____
- ☐ _____
- ☐ _____
- ☐ _____

Games & Activities
- ☐ Poster board
- ☐ Markers, pencils
- ☐ Construction paper
- ☐ Scissors, tape, string
- ☐ Paper
- ☐ CDs or cassettes, CD or cassette player
- ☐ _____
- ☐ _____
- ☐ _____
- ☐ _____
- ☐ _____

Food & Juice or Soft Drinks
- ☐ _____
- ☐ _____
- ☐ _____
- ☐ _____

Paper Products
- ☐ Paper plates
- ☐ Paper cups
- ☐ Napkins
- ☐ Table covering
- ☐ Plastic tableware
- ☐ Trash bags
- ☐ _____
- ☐ _____

Party Favors
- ☐ _____
- ☐ _____

Other Items
- ☐ Camera and film
- ☐ _____
- ☐ _____
- ☐ _____
- ☐ _____

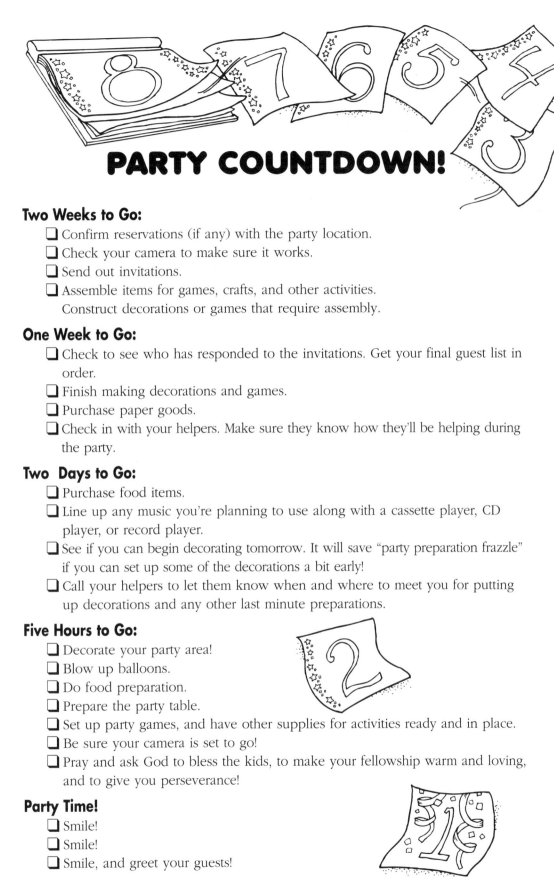

PARTY COUNTDOWN!

Two Weeks to Go:
- ❑ Confirm reservations (if any) with the party location.
- ❑ Check your camera to make sure it works.
- ❑ Send out invitations.
- ❑ Assemble items for games, crafts, and other activities.
  Construct decorations or games that require assembly.

One Week to Go:
- ❑ Check to see who has responded to the invitations. Get your final guest list in order.
- ❑ Finish making decorations and games.
- ❑ Purchase paper goods.
- ❑ Check in with your helpers. Make sure they know how they'll be helping during the party.

Two Days to Go:
- ❑ Purchase food items.
- ❑ Line up any music you're planning to use along with a cassette player, CD player, or record player.
- ❑ See if you can begin decorating tomorrow. It will save "party preparation frazzle" if you can set up some of the decorations a bit early!
- ❑ Call your helpers to let them know when and where to meet you for putting up decorations and any other last minute preparations.

Five Hours to Go:
- ❑ Decorate your party area!
- ❑ Blow up balloons.
- ❑ Do food preparation.
- ❑ Prepare the party table.
- ❑ Set up party games, and have other supplies for activities ready and in place.
- ❑ Be sure your camera is set to go!
- ❑ Pray and ask God to bless the kids, to make your fellowship warm and loving, and to give you perseverance!

Party Time!
- ❑ Smile!
- ❑ Smile!
- ❑ Smile, and greet your guests!

GAMES & ACTIVITIES LIST

Theme: _____ (p._____)

Games: **Need to Buy:**

1._____   _____

2._____   _____

3._____   _____

4._____   _____

5._____   _____

Craft Activity: **Need to Buy:**

1._____   _____

Other Activities: **Need to Buy:**

1._____   _____

2._____   _____

3._____   _____

4._____   _____

LAST MINUTE PARTY POINTERS

These last minute "helps" will help you sail through parties and special events with flying colors. So celebrate! Try something new! Be creative! And rejoice in fellowship and fun with God's most precious treasure—his children!

● Think your celebration through from the standpoint of the guests. Are the decorations inviting? Do you have a good selection of activities? Will the party create happy memories for children to take home?

● Plan to have a variety of active games as well as quieter activities, such as craft projects for kids who are less kinesthetic. Be sensitive to kids' varying needs.

● Plan a few more activities than you'll actually need. It's always easier to drop an activity or two than to scramble for ideas while the party is in progress.

● Tie games, activities, crafts, and snacks into your party theme. If you're drawing ideas from this book to create your own, original parties, be sure to rename games and create different props to accompany the theme you've chosen.

● Keep ooey-gooey sweets to a minimum—but don't neglect offering them! Kids look disdainfully at sunflower seeds and carrot juice for party treats! Fruits, vegetables and dips, finger sandwiches, and fruit punch are good alternatives if you want to steer clear of cookies and cake.

● Ask teenagers to help at your parties. They're full of energy, and most teens enjoy "being a kid again" in a party setting!

● Keep in mind kids' ages as you plan games, crafts, and other activities. Remember, the younger the child the shorter the attention span. Long, involved games and activities result in boredom and frustration for little ones.

● Offer games that include *all* the children and that focus on fun rather than winning. If you do offer treats or small prizes, make sure everyone gets the same type of prize.

● If your party is inside, plan to go outside for games that involve races and running. If you must stay inside, modify running games by having children hop or crawl.

● Steer clear of elimination games, such as Musical Chairs. They make kids feel left out and restless—especially if the game lasts a long time.

● Assemble a Party Props box to keep common party supplies at your fingertips. Collect the following items and store them in a decorated box:

  ✔ rolls of colorful crepe paper,
  ✔ a bag of balloons,
  ✔ tape,
  ✔ scissors,
  ✔ a bag of self-adhesive bows,
  ✔ a bag of confetti, and
  ✔ a spool of curling ribbon.

With your Party Props box close at hand, you'll always be ready for birthdays, special events, and spur-of-the-moment get-togethers!

● Expect the unexpected and have fun anyway. The best-planned party may have its bumps, but keeping a positive outlook and ready sense of humor will help you smooth over the roughest spots.

Now ... *let's PARTY!*

Hula Hula-Baloo

Take a party break and "head to the islands" for festive, tropical fun!

The Theme
A tropical "get-away" adventure

PARTY PREPARATIONS

Invitations

● Make photocopies of the Pineapple pattern on page 18 onto stiff paper, then color and cut out the patterns. Fill out party information in the spaces provided. Slip colorful silk flowers in the envelopes along with the invitations. Mail or hand out the invitations.

Decorations

● Make perky palm trees to "plant" around your party area. Twist brown paper grocery sacks into tree trunks, then tape them to the walls to create 5-foot-tall trees. Tear large palm leaves from green construction paper, then tape the leaves to the tree trunks on the walls. Be sure some of the leaves drape over the trunks. For an extra fun touch, place a few real pineapples around the trees.

● String fishing net or yarn from the ceiling. Toss balloon "fish" in the "nets." You may wish to decorate the balloons by taping on construction paper fins and using a black marker to add faces. Use the "fishaloons" as party favors for kids to take as they leave.

● Tape bright paper, silk, or fabric flowers around the room.

● Add blue crepe paper "waves" along the edge of the food table, wall, or door. You may want to set a fan under the table to make the waves ripple.

● Collect a cassette tape of Hawaiian music and a cassette player. (You can find recordings of Hawaiian ukulele music at most public libraries.) Play Hawaiian music as kids arrive to get them in an "island mood"!

GAMES GALORE

Lively Leis *(icebreaker)*

Before the party, purchase bright silk flowers and pull them from their stems. You'll need five "blossoms" and a 20-inch length of fishing line for each person.

As kids arrive, greet them with a friendly "aloha," and hand them each a length of fishing line and five silk flowers. Have kids trade their flowers with others as they exchange names. When everyone has traded a flower with each of the other guests, have kids help each other tie the ends of their fishing lines together to create leis to wear.

Jimbo Limbo (game)

Before the party, wrap blue crepe paper around a broom handle or 1-inch dowel. Play a cassette tape or CD of lively Hawaiian music during this high-energy game.

Choose two kids to hold the ends of the broom handle. Have the rest of the kids line up on one side of the broom handle. Explain that each time they "limbo" under the stick without touching it, they can shout "jimbo!" When kids touch the stick, let them try again. See how "low you can go" before everyone misses.

Coconut Relay Roll (game)

You'll need two coconuts or balloons for this game. Have kids form two lines, and hand the first person in each line a coconut. Tell kids that the object of the game is to roll the coconut (or bop the balloon) between their legs down each line until the player at the back gets it. Those players will then run with the coconuts to the front of their lines and begin rolling the coconuts through the lines again. Continue playing until the first player from one group returns to the head of the line. Give coconut candy bars or macaroon cookies to all the players as coco-"nutty" prizes!

Seashell Sculpting (craft)

Before the party, purchase a bag of seashells from a craft or hobby store. Cover a table with newspaper, then set out the seashells and tacky craft glue. Let kids "hunt" for their favorite shells, then glue them together to create unusual sculptures. As an option, you might want to provide self-adhesive magnetic strips or let kids look for twigs to add to their sculptures. Encourage kids to use their creations at home as table decorations or paperweights.

TREAT TO EAT

Island Cookies

Set out marshmallow creme, blue decorative sprinkles, plastic knives, chocolate kisses, and a plate of rice cakes. Have kids spread a thin layer of marshmallow creme on their rice cakes, then sprinkle blue "ocean waves" on top. Add chocolate kiss "islands" in the centers of the rice cakes.

Maui Powie Punch

Mix fruit punch and lemon-lime soda in a large bowl. Add a large scoop of pineapple sherbet to the punch. For a festive touch, float a silk flower or two in the punch bowl. You might also consider buying tiny party umbrellas to add to each guest's paper cup!

PARTY PARTINGS

Talk to the children individually as they leave, and express your joy at having each one attend the party. Remind kids that God is with them wherever they go—the mountains, the seashore, and even tropical islands. Hand each child a palm leaf cut from green construction paper. Let them wave their palm leaves and say "aloha" as they leave. Be sure kids take their seashell sculptures and leis home.

SHOPPING LIST FOR HULA HULA-BALOO

Invitations
- ☐ silk flowers (also used in Decorations and Games Galore)
- ☐ envelopes and stamps

Decorations
- ☐ brown paper grocery sacks
- ☐ masking tape
- ☐ green construction paper (also used in Party Partings)
- ☐ fishing net
- ☐ balloons

- ☐ blue crepe paper (also used in Games Galore)
- ☐ cassette tape of Hawaiian music and cassette player (also used in Games Galore)

Games & Activities
- ☐ fishing line
- ☐ broom handle
- ☐ two coconuts
- ☐ coconut candy bars
- ☐ bag of seashells
- ☐ newspaper

- ☐ tacky craft glue

Foods & Tableware
- ☐ marshmallow creme
- ☐ blue decorative sprinkles
- ☐ chocolate kisses
- ☐ rice cakes
- ☐ fruit punch
- ☐ lemon-lime soda
- ☐ pineapple sherbet
- ☐ plastic knives, napkins, and paper cups

You're
Invited
to a
HULA
HULA-BALOO!

When: _____

Where: _____ To: _____

From: _____

Wear brightly
colored clothing!

The Theme
Ducks and geese

Wacky Waddler Party

Kids may think you've gone "quackers" with this party—but they'll love it! Plan this as a summer celebration, or use it in the fall when ducks are migrating south—and kids are migrating back to your class!

PARTY PREPARATIONS

Invitations

● Photocopy the Duck pattern on page 23 onto yellow paper. Glue a few craft feathers on the ducks' tails, then fill in the party information. Mail or hand out the invitations.

Decorations

● Place a plastic tablecloth on the floor in one corner of your party area. Set a large tub partially filled with water on the tablecloth. If this is a summer party, consider holding the event outside and providing a partially filled wading pool instead of a tub. Purchase a small, rubber duck for each guest. Or make your own floating ducks inexpensively by drawing and photocopying small ducks using the invitation pattern as a guide. Then cut out the patterns and tape them so that they stand upright on plastic lids. Set the ducks afloat in the tub or wading pool.

Teacher Tip

Always watch children carefully when doing water activities.

● Scatter craft feathers around your party area.

● Photocopy the Duck pattern on page 23, making sure to cover the words. Color the pattern, cut it out, and tape it to a wall as a Wacky Waddler wall decoration. If you're really feeling "quackers," make extra photocopies of the Duck pattern and hang them from the ceiling using fishing line or string. Add a few craft feathers for a great effect.

● A duck call (found in most sporting goods stores) makes a novel way to welcome guests and serves as a great attention-getting signal during games and activities.

GAMES GALORE

Duck Hats (icebreaker)

Set out paper cups, markers, craft feathers, tape, and orange construction paper. As guests arrive, have them find partners and work together to create duck hats. Have kids turn their cups upside down and draw eyes on them. Then show kids how to cut or tear duckbills from the orange construction paper and tape the bills to the bottom edges of the cups. Let kids stick a few craft feathers on the tops of their hats. Have kids gently tape the finished duck hats on their heads, then greet the other "quackers" in the flock.

Flying in Formation (game)

This silly race requires kids to cooperate with their "flocks." Before the party, blow up and tie off a balloon for each player. Form two flocks and hand each "duck" a balloon. Have ducks position the balloons between their knees. Create a "flying formation" by having one child in each flock be the Lead Duck. Have two ducks stand behind the Lead Duck, then make a row of three ducks, and so on until each flock is in a triangular formation.

Tell ducks that they must keep the balloons between their knees as they waddle to the opposite end of the party area. They must stay in formation unless you call out, "Change leaders." Then another duck in the flock can move into the leader position as everyone else falls into formation again. Call out directions such as "Left turn" or "Right turn" as the ducks are flying to their destination. When they reach the other end of the party area, have them change leaders and return to the starting place. After the game, hand each duck a "quispy quacker" (cracker) as a silly prize! Save the balloons for the next game.

Goose Egg (game)

Have kids form two groups. Hand each child a sheet of newspaper and a balloon "goose egg." Tell kids the object of the game is for them to waddle to the opposite end of the party area with their balloons between their legs, to make a nest by crumpling their newspaper, then sit on their eggs and "hatch" (pop) them. The group that hatches all their eggs first can shout "honk!"

Begin the game by saying "go." When one group shouts "honk," stop the game, and let the members of the winning group each choose a hard-boiled egg as a prize. Then let the members of the other group each choose an egg. If you hold this party in the spring, you may want to substitute chocolate eggs for hard-boiled eggs.

Pin the Tail Feather on the Duck *(game)*

This quick game is played just like the old party classic Pin the Tail on the Donkey. Use craft feathers and the Wacky Waddler wall decoration. Blindfold your guests, then let them take turns taping craft feathers on the duck. The player whose feather is closest to the duck's tail receives his or her choice of the craft feathers as a prize. Be sure to let the other players each choose a fluffy feather, too!

Duck Races *(activity)*

Have each child choose a rubber duck to race from the "duck pond." Then have kids take turns racing their ducks in pairs. Have two kids place their ducks at one end of the duck pond, then blow their ducks across the water. Let the child whose duck is first to reach the opposite side of the pond take his or her choice of five jelly bean eggs. Then have the runner-up choose five jelly bean eggs.

Feather Paintings *(craft)*

Cover a table with newspaper. Set out bowls of water, craft feathers, white paper, and watercolor paint boxes. Let guests each choose a feather "brush" to paint with. Challenge kids to paint pictures of the silliest ducks or geese their imaginations can "hatch"!

TREAT TO EAT

Duck Doughnuts

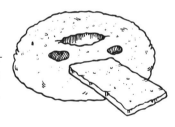

Provide large, powdered sugar doughnuts, graham crackers, and raisins. Invite guests to create daffy-looking doughnut ducks by sticking graham cracker halves in the doughnuts as duckbills, then adding raisin eyes.

Goose Juice

Before the party, cut or tear webbed feet from orange construction paper. Tape the webbed feet on the bottoms of paper cups. Prepare goose juice by mixing apple juice and a bit of cinnamon in a large bowl. For extra fun, float a toy duck in the party bowl!

PARTY PARTINGS

As guests leave, hand out craft feathers, and express your happiness that they came and enjoyed the party. Mention that just as ducks and geese flock together, God's people are a flock who help each other too. You may wish to let each child choose a rubber duck from the duck pond to take home as a special party favor.

SHOPPING LIST
FOR WACKY WADDLER PARTY

Invitations
- ❑ craft feathers (also used in Decorations, Games Galore, and Party Partings)
- ❑ envelopes and stamps

Decorations
- ❑ plastic tablecloth
- ❑ large tub
- ❑ small, rubber ducks

Games & Activities
- ❑ paper cups (also used in Treat to Eat)
- ❑ orange construction paper (also used in Treat to Eat)
- ❑ balloons
- ❑ crackers
- ❑ newspaper
- ❑ hard-boiled eggs
- ❑ jelly bean eggs
- ❑ plastic bowls for water
- ❑ white paper
- ❑ watercolor paint boxes
- ❑ blindfold

Foods & Tableware
- ❑ large, powdered sugar donuts
- ❑ graham crackers
- ❑ raisins
- ❑ apple juice
- ❑ cinnamon
- ❑ napkins

IT'S A
WACKY WADDLER
PARTY!

When: _____

Where: _____

From: _____ To: _____

Bring a
"Ducky" Friend!

Pillow Party

The Theme

A slumber party

You won't be caught dozing with this super celebration! This fun overnight get-together works for boys or girls and makes a great preteen lock-in party.

PARTY PREPARATIONS

Invitations

● Photocopy the Pillow pattern on page 27. Fill in the party information, then fold on the dotted line and tape two of the sides closed. Carefully stuff the invitation with paper towels or facial tissue, then tape the last side of the "pillow" closed. Mail or hand out the invitations.

Decorations

● Scatter a variety of pillows around the party area.

● Drape colorful blankets and quilts over tables and chairs. You may wish to provide a few stuffed animals by the blankets.

● Hang twinkling Christmas tree lights around the party area on the walls, door frames, and windows.

● Use fishing line to suspend glow-in-the-dark stars from the ceiling. Or make your own stars from stiff paper, and add glitter around the edges.

GAMES GALORE

Pillow Pals *(icebreaker)*

Before the party, cut two 5-inch felt squares for each guest. Use several different colors of felt.

As guests arrive, hand them each two different colored felt "pillows," and challenge them to find the matching pillows. When the matching pillows are found, have kids tell each other their names, then stuff their pillows with paper towels or facial tissue and staple them closed. Take each guest's picture now or at some time during the party. Save the pictures for the Party Partings.

Pillow-in-the-Dark *(game)*

Kids will need to use their own full-sized pillow to play this game. Choose one child to be the Shiner, and hand him or her a flashlight. Tell kids that this game is played in the dark and that the object of the game is to hide their pillows from the Shiner's light. If the Shiner shines a light on a pillow, he or she hands the flashlight to that person who then becomes the next Shiner.

Make-the-Bed Relay *(game)*

For this game, you'll need two bedsheets, two blankets, and two pillows. Place both sets of bedding at one end of the party area. Form two lines opposite the sets of bedding. Have the first person in each line hop across the party area, spread out the sheet, lay the blanket on top, then add the pillow. He or she then hops back to the line, and the next person hops to the "bed," ruffles it up, then remakes it. The first group finished receives their choice of fruit leather "blankets" to eat. Be sure the other group members each get edible blankets, too!

Shadow Charades *(activity)*

For this activity you'll need a flashlight and a bedsheet or a large piece of poster board. Tape the bedsheet or poster board on a wall.

Have kids form pairs, then hand the flashlight to one pair. Have one partner hold the flashlight while the other partner makes shadow shapes on the wall. Whisper the name of an animal or other object to both partners. The pair will then have one minute to make the shadow shape on the wall while the rest of the pairs guess what it is. If a pair guesses correctly, they become the next shadow-makers. If no one guesses correctly after one minute, tell them what the shadow was and choose another pair of shadow-makers. Continue until each pair has had a turn being shadow-makers.

Glow-in-the-Dark Rings *(craft)*

Before the party, cut ½×3-inch strips of poster board. You'll need one strip for each guest. Purchase one or two packages of glow-in-the-dark stickers.

Set out the stickers, tape, and poster board strips. Have kids get with their Pillow Pals to make rings. Encourage kids to help each other fit a strip around one finger, then tape it into a ring. Have them use stickers to decorate their rings. When kids are finished, let them hold their rings by a flashlight or lamp. Then turn out the lights, and let kids admire the "glowing" results!

TREAT TO EAT

Pizza Pillows

Purchase frozen pizza rolls or let kids have fun making them, using pizza sauce, grated mozzarella cheese, and refrigerator biscuit dough. Show kids how to flatten a biscuit, place a spoonful of pizza sauce and cheese in the center, then lay another biscuit on top and seal the edges with fork tines. Bake at 350 degrees until golden brown.

Slumber Soda

Serve chilled apple juice. Let kids make fancy cup decorations by sliding large, pillowy marshmallows on drinking straws.

PARTY PARTINGS

Before the party, photocopy the "Good Morning, Sunshine!" Picture Frame pattern on page 28 onto stiff yellow paper. Cut out a frame for each guest, then cut out the center of the sun.

Before guests leave, serve doughnut holes, fruit juice, and milk. Tape the children's photographs behind the openings in the sun on the picture frames. As kids leave, give them the picture frames to remember their special night of fun—and give them each a joyous hug to celebrate God's new day!

SHOPPING LIST
FOR PILLOW PARTY

Invitations
- ❑ paper towels or facial tissues (also used in Games Galore)
- ❑ envelopes and stamps

Decorations
- ❑ pillows (also used in Games Galore)
- ❑ blankets and quilts
- ❑ twinkling Christmas tree lights
- ❑ fishing line
- ❑ glow-in-the-dark stars

Games & Activities
- ❑ felt
- ❑ full-sized pillow for each child
- ❑ flashlight
- ❑ two bedsheets
- ❑ two blankets
- ❑ fruit leathers
- ❑ poster board
- ❑ glow-in-the-dark stickers
- ❑ instant-print camera (also used in Party Partings)

Foods & Tableware
- ❑ frozen pizza rolls (or see Treat to Eat for recipe)
- ❑ apple juice
- ❑ large marshmallows
- ❑ drinking straws
- ❑ napkins and paper cups

Party Partings
- ❑ doughnut holes
- ❑ fruit juices
- ❑ milk

Pillow Party!

You're invited to a:

ZZZZZ ZZZ

When: _____

Where: _____

From: _____ To: _____

Bring pj's, a sleeping bag, and your favorite pillow!

fold here

Not-So-Starving Artists' Party

Center a celebration around arts and crafts projects and your party will paint a thousand words—of joy!

The Theme

Arts and crafts

Party Preparations

Invitations
● Photocopy the Palette pattern on page 33 onto stiff paper for each guest. Cut out the patterns, and fill in the party information. Color the "paint splotches" on the invitations with bright markers. Mail or hand out the invitations.

Decorations
● Stack empty paint cans around your party area.

● Cover the floor under craft tables with plastic dropcloths, newspaper, or old bedsheets. Your cleanup will be a snap, and you won't have to worry about spills and spots!

● Tie colorful bows around inexpensive paintbrushes, then hang them from the ceiling. Use the paintbrushes as take-home party favors for Party Partings.

● Create two large poster board palettes using the Palette pattern on page 33 as a guide. Cut out the palettes, but don't color paint splotches on them. Hang the blank palettes on a wall to use during the party.

● You may want to hang extra paint shirts on hangers around your party area in case some kids forget to bring old shirts. Check used clothing stores for inexpensive men's shirts. Make the shirts exciting and inviting by splashing dabs of paint on them prior to the party.

● Hang brightly colored crepe paper streamers around the party area.

GAMES GALORE

Palette Partners *(icebreaker)*

Before the party, cut pairs of red, blue, yellow, orange, purple, and green "paint splotches" from construction paper. Hand each guest a paint splotch as he or she arrives. Have kids form trios with others whose paint splotches are closely related colors. Some combinations might be red, yellow, and orange; yellow, green, and blue; or red, blue, and purple. When color families are formed, have kids tape their color splotches to the blank palettes on the wall then write their names on the splotches.

Light Up Your Life *(craft)*

Set out permanent markers; glitter; white craft glue; and white, plastic light switch plates. Plastic switch plates are available at any hardware store or discount center and are very inexpensive.

Invite kids to decorate the light switch plates with their choice of designs. You might offer ideas such as pictures of Jesus, special friends, flowers, stars, hearts, or rockets. Encourage kids to use lots of color, then add glitter for sparkly fun. Suggest that kids ask their parents to help them put up their light switch plates in their bedrooms at home. (Emphasize that they should never remove or replace switch plates on their own!)

Sand Painting *(craft)*

Set out bowls of table salt, plastic spoons, a box of colored sidewalk chalk, white craft glue, and empty baby food jars with lids. You'll need one baby food jar and lid for each guest. Show kids how to make colored "sand" by rubbing sidewalk chalk around and around in each bowl of salt. The more kids rub the chalk in the salt, the brighter the sand will become. Add glitter to the salt if you want a little sparkle in the sand. Let kids spoon the tinted sand into their jars in colorful layers. Demonstrate how to push a toothpick down through the sand layers to create designs along the edges of the jar. When the designs are completed, have kids spread glue along the inside rims of the jar lids then screw the lids on the jars securely. Remind kids to avoid shaking their jars so their designs will remain intact.

Nature Sculptures *(craft)*

Set out a variety of items from nature, such as twigs, interesting leaves, flower buds, seashells, tiny pine cones, dried thistles, and colorful pebbles. Hand each child a piece of aluminum foil and a small lump of self-hardening clay. Instruct kids to flatten the clay with their hands into ¼-inch thicknesses then place the clay on the foil squares. Let kids choose nature items to press into the clay. Kids may leave the items in the clay or press and remove them to make nature prints. Tell kids the clay will air-dry in about 24 hours.

Jelly Bean Jamboree *(game)*

Have kids play this game as their art projects dry. Hand each child a plastic sandwich bag containing 12 colored jelly beans. Tell kids they'll have 30 seconds to make as many same-colored pairs as they can by trading jelly beans with others. At the end of 30 seconds, count to see who has the most pairs. Have kids play once more but see if they can make "foursies." Hand out fresh jelly beans to nibble after the game.

TREAT TO EAT

Sandwich Sculptures

Set out paper plates, slices of bread, cookie cutters, plastic knives, lettuce, slices of ham and cheese, peanut butter and jelly, mustard, and olives. Encourage kids to sculpt their own edible creations.

Paint Punch

Mix fruit punch and apple juice. Serve the punch in brightly colored paper cups. For extra fun, use bright, inexpensive plastic mugs or cups, then let kids take them home to decorate. You may wish to mix your punch in a bright plastic "paint" bucket!

Party Partings

Gather kids and express your joy at sharing this party with them. Remind them that it was God's creativity that made each person so special. Hand out bags of colored jelly beans, gummy candies, or gumdrops. Tie the treat bags with bright bows. Hand out grocery bags for guests to use to transport their art projects safely home.

SHOPPING LIST
FOR NOT-SO-STARVING ARTISTS' PARTY

Invitations
- [ ] envelopes and stamps

Decorations
- [ ] empty paint cans
- [ ] plastic dropcloths
- [ ] ribbon (also used in Party Partings)
- [ ] small paintbrushes
- [ ] poster board
- [ ] men's old shirts (for extra paint shirts)
- [ ] crepe paper

Games & Activities
- [ ] red, blue, yellow, orange, purple, and green construction paper
- [ ] permanent markers
- [ ] glitter
- [ ] white, plastic light switch plates
- [ ] table salt
- [ ] plastic spoons
- [ ] colored sidewalk chalk
- [ ] empty baby food jars with lids
- [ ] toothpicks
- [ ] nature items, such as twigs, pebbles, seashells, and leaves
- [ ] aluminum foil
- [ ] self-hardening clay
- [ ] jelly beans (also used in Party Partings)
- [ ] plastic sandwich bags (also used in Party Partings)

Foods & Tableware
- [ ] bread
- [ ] cookie cutters
- [ ] lettuce
- [ ] ham and cheese slices
- [ ] peanut butter and jelly
- [ ] fruit punch and apple juice
- [ ] condiments
- [ ] paper plates, paper cups, plastic knives, and napkins

Party Partings
- [ ] paper grocery sacks

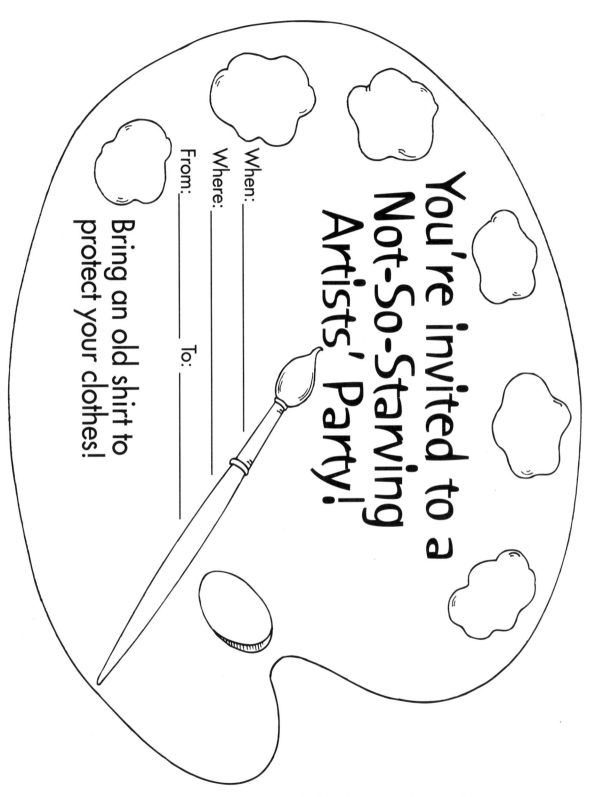

You're invited to a Not-So-Starving Artists' Party!

When:

Where:

From: _____ To: _____

Bring an old shirt to protect your clothes!

Pass It On Party

The Theme

Serving others

Celebrate the gift of helping others. Use these community projects to help others—and party—all year long!

PARTY PREPARATIONS

Invitations

Choose a project as a focus for your party, and note on the invitations the items guests are to bring from the following suggestions:

- **January**—storybooks for children's home or state hospital; bring a small picture book
- **February**—greeting cards for hospitals or nursing homes; bring a colorful greeting card
- **March**—money for missionaries; bring coins to put in a giant piggy bank
- **April**—sweet treats for the elderly; bring an edible treat for someone
- **May**—flowers for care centers or hospice centers; bring a flower or a small potted plant
- **June**—yardwork for elderly or disabled homeowners; bring a trash bag and garden tool to use
- **July**—"Christmas in July" for the needy; bring a gift to wrap
- **August**—school supplies for missionaries; bring school supplies to be sent to missionaries to use in their schools and churches
- **September**—warm clothes for the needy; bring a new or gently used article of warm clothing, such as a coat, a sweater, socks, mittens, a hat, or a scarf
- **October**—blanket drive for the needy and elderly; bring a new or gently used blanket or quilt
- **November**—Food for families in need; bring a canned or boxed food item
- **December**—toys for children; bring a new or gently used toy or game to wrap

After you've chosen a party theme, photocopy the Heart pattern on page 37 onto pink paper. Fill in the party information. You may want to include a few small candy hearts in each envelope. Mail or hand out the invitations.

Decorations

● Select your party decorations according to the party theme you've chosen. For instance, you might hang play money from the ceiling for the missionaries' money party or dress stuffed garbage bag "snowmen" for the warm clothing party. Add lots of cutout hearts around the party area.

● Make life-sized paper dolls from white shelf paper to hang on the walls. Be sure they have big smiles and hearts!

GAMES GALORE

All the games and activities are focused on helping each other—the theme of any project you've chosen for your party!

Party Dolls *(icebreaker)*

Provide colorful markers, and encourage guests to decorate and sign their names on the life-sized paper dolls. As kids work together, ask them to think of the people this party will help. Remind kids how happy it makes everyone when we share the good things God gives us.

Partner Dodge Ball *(game)*

This is a good outside game, but it can be played inside in an open area if you use a foam ball. Form two groups, and have the kids in each group find partners. Designate a center line. Tell kids they must link elbows with their partners to play. Players will toss the ball back and forth and try to keep from being tagged by the ball. Partners who are tagged must hold their hands in the air. When both partners are tagged, the pair "freezes" until another pair from their group taps them on the shoulders to "unfreeze" them. Encourage kids to cooperate and help each other. Give gumballs to everyone as prizes.

Help Me, Help You *(game)*

Form a circle. If you have more than 10 kids, form two or three circles. Have kids use large rubber bands to connect their wrists with the people on either side. When each circle is completely connected, set paper and markers in the center of each circle. Ask kids to draw four pictures: a picture of someone helping another person, a picture of a person smiling, a picture of people holding hands, and a picture of the world. Encourage kids to work cooperatively. When the pictures are finished, have kids remove the rubber bands from their wrists, then talk about what it was like to work with each other so closely. Hold up the completed pictures, and explain that working together to help others makes everyone happy and brings us closer to people all over the world!

Wrap Up *(activity)*

Provide gift wrap, tape, self-adhesive bows, and scissors. Have the kids wrap the gifts they brought as donations then decorate a large box and pile the wrapped gifts inside. Assure your guests that you'll get their gifts to the people who need them.

TREAT TO EAT

Heart Cookies

Set out napkins, sugar cookies, canned icing, plastic knives, and candy sprinkles. Have some kids be frosting spreaders and others be sprinklers. Encourage kids to help each other create delicious cookies to share.

Strawberry Punch

Mix up a pitcher of strawberry or cherry soft drink mix. Add lots of ice cubes, then float sliced strawberries in the punch.

PARTY PARTINGS

Before the party, purchase small wooden hearts at a craft or hobby store. Buy one heart for each guest. Paint the hearts in neon colors, then use a permanent marker to write, "Jesus loves _____" on each heart. At the party's close, let each guest choose a heart and write his or her name in the blank. As kids fill in their names, affirm them for showing Jesus' love in practical ways by helping others.

SHOPPING LIST
FOR PASS IT ON PARTY

Invitations
- ☐ envelopes and stamps

Decorations
- ☐ white shelf paper (also used in Games Galore)

Games & Activities
- ☐ playground ball
- ☐ gumballs

- ☐ large rubber bands
- ☐ paper
- ☐ gift wrap
- ☐ self-adhesive bows
- ☐ large box

Foods & Tableware
- ☐ sugar cookies
- ☐ canned icing
- ☐ candy sprinkles
- ☐ strawberry soft drink mix
- ☐ strawberries
- ☐ napkins, plastic knives, and paper cups

Party Partings
- ☐ small wooden hearts
- ☐ neon colored craft paints
- ☐ permanent marker

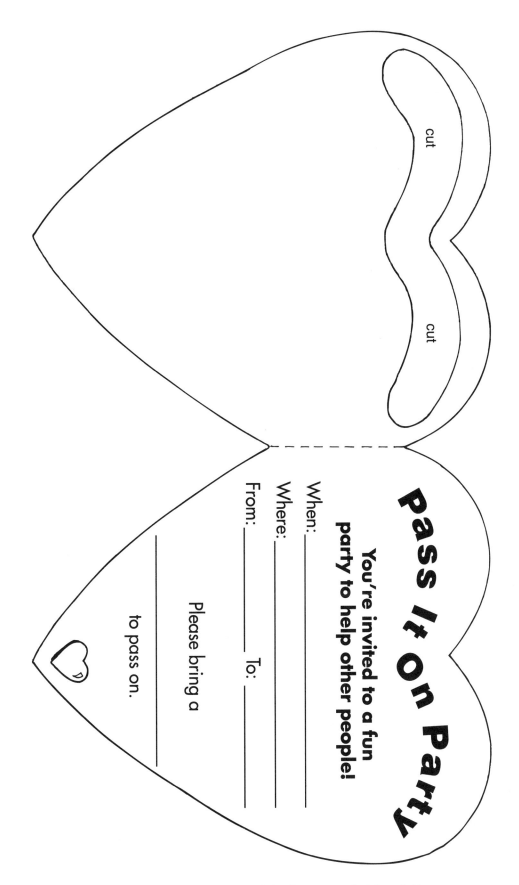

cut

cut

Pass It On Party

You're invited to a fun party to help other people!

When: _____

Where: _____

From: _____ To: _____

Please bring a _____ to pass on.

The Instant Party

The Theme
An impromptu celebration

Collect party items, add one group of lively kids, mix them together and . . . voilà—instant party fun!

PARTY PREPARATIONS

Invitations

● You won't need invitations! The fun of this party theme is in its spontaneity. *You* can gather the party items in advance—but let the kids feel the excitement of a spur-of-the-moment celebration.

● Collect all the party items suggested on the Shopping List. After kids arrive at your room, tell them you're all going to celebrate just being together! Have kids form three groups: the Interior Decorators, the Game Group, and the Treat Team. The Interior Decorators will be in charge of decking the halls with the items you've provided. The Game Group can use the game items to invent fun games to play as an entire group. And the Treat Team is in charge of making yummy delectables with the foods you've provided. Give teams 10 or 15 minutes to "do their thing," then let the celebration begin!

Decorations

● Decorating suggestions: Hang crepe paper streamers, sprinkle a little confetti in balloons then blow them up, scatter bits of confetti on the treat table.

GAMES GALORE

Game suggestions: Dodge Ball; Pass-the-Balloon relays; Beanbag Toss, using empty milk cartons; and Balloon Volleyball.

TREAT TO EAT

Treat suggestions: Frost and decorate cupcakes, and decorate napkins and cups with markers.

PARTY PARTINGS

Gather kids at the end of the party. Express your delight at how well everyone worked together to make the celebration so much fun. Point out that when we work together in God's love, great things are accomplished! Let kids take balloons and crepe paper streamers home as impromptu party favors.

SHOPPING LIST
FOR THE INSTANT PARTY

Decorations
- ❏ crepe paper
- ❏ confetti
- ❏ balloons

Games & Activities
- ❏ playground ball

- ❏ balloons
- ❏ beanbags
- ❏ empty milk cartons

Foods & Tableware
- ❏ cupcakes
- ❏ canned icing

- ❏ raisins, peanuts, and miniature marshmallows
- ❏ apple juice
- ❏ napkins, plastic knives, and paper cups

Jungle Jamboree

The Theme

Jungle animals

Let your kids turn into big time game hunters and "bag" some big time fun!

PARTY PREPARATIONS

Invitations

● Photocopy the Party Monkey pattern on page 43 onto stiff brown paper. Cut out an invitation for each guest, and fill in the party information. Accordion fold the monkeys' tails. You may wish to photocopy and include the Coupon for free bananas on page 43. Mail or hand out the invitations.

Decorations

● Scatter a variety of stuffed animals around the party area.

● Enlarge the Tropical Leaf pattern on page 44, then use the pattern as a guide to cut LOTS of leaves from green construction paper. Snip the edges to give them a fringed look. Hang the leaves from the ceiling, lamps, above doors and windows, and along the party table. You may wish to twist brown paper grocery sacks and tape them to the walls as tree trunks, then add clusters of leaves at the top.

● Hang twisted "vines" of brown and green crepe paper from the ceiling.

● Add splashes of color with bright yellow, red, and orange balloons.

● Cut animal, bird, or fish pictures out of magazines or photocopy and color the Animal patterns on page 44. Tape the pictures around the room.

GAMES GALORE

Pith Helmets *(icebreaker)*

Set out paper bowls and green, black, and brown markers. As kids arrive, have them each find a "hunting partner." Tell the partners to create pith helmets by coloring the bowls in a camouflage pattern. Have them place the finished helmets on their heads then find another pair of big game hunters and learn one another's names. Be sure to hand out bananas to kids if you included the Coupons for free bananas in the invitations.

Tiger Tail *(game)*

Before the party, cut a 10-inch-long "tiger tail" from fake fur or felt for each child. Have kids slip the tails in their waistbands or under their belts in back. If some kids aren't wearing clothing with waistbands or belts, use masking tape to attach their tails. On "go," have kids try to snatch one another's tiger tails without losing their own. After 15 seconds, call time and see who still has their tiger tails attached.

Then play an alternate form of the same game. Have kids form two lines with each person holding the shoulders of the person in front. Have the last person in each line attach a tiger tail to his or her waistband. On "go," have groups try to snatch each other's tail.

Let kids keep their tiger tails as party favors.

Safari Hunt *(game)*

Make sure you've scattered stuffed animals and taped animal pictures around the room. Have kids get with their hunting partners. Hand each pair paper and pencils. Tell kids that they're going on a big game hunt and that they must draw as many animals, birds, and fish as they can in two minutes. After time is up, have pairs count the animals they "bagged," then hand each child a box of animal crackers as a prize.

Squirt Those Critters *(game)*

Photocopy the Animal patterns on page 44. Color and cut out the patterns, then tape them to paper cups.

Spread a plastic tablecloth on the floor and part way up a wall. Tape the tablecloth in place. Line up the animal cups against a wall. Let kids take turns using water pistols to give the animals a "shower." Allow each child six squirts of the water pistol. Each time an animal is hit, score 1 point. Each time an animal is tipped over, score 2 points. When everyone has had a chance to squirt the animals, total the points. Let the person with the most points choose a toy plastic monkey or banana as a prize. Then let the rest of the "hunters" choose prizes.

Native Necklaces *(craft)*

Before the party, purchase leather shoelaces in 20-inch lengths. Set out different kinds of craft beads and craft feathers. Let kids string beads and tie feathers onto the leather shoelaces then tie the ends together to create nifty native necklaces to wear. Give kids the option of cutting their shoelaces in half to create bracelets rather than necklaces.

TREAT TO EAT

Leopard Cookies

Set out napkins, graham crackers, plastic knives, white canned icing, and a bowl of chocolate chips. Let kids spread icing on the graham crackers, then add chocolate chip "leopard spots."

Safari Sodas

Place a scoop of orange sherbet or sorbet in each paper cup, then add pineapple juice. Add a plastic spoon and drinking straw to each cup. For a tropical touch, top off the sherbet with a silk flower.

PARTY PARTINGS

At the party's end, mention how many beautiful creatures God has made to roam in the jungle and all around the world. Point out that it is important to care for God's world and all the creatures in it. Hand each child an animal-shaped eraser or animal sticker page as he or she is leaving. Be sure to express your joy at seeing each child!

SHOPPING LIST
FOR JUNGLE JAMBOREE

Invitations
- ❑ envelopes and stamps

Decorations
- ❑ stuffed animals (also used in Games Galore)
- ❑ green construction paper
- ❑ brown and green crepe paper
- ❑ bright yellow, red, and orange balloons
- ❑ animal pictures from magazines

Games & Activities
- ❑ paper bowls
- ❑ green, black, and brown markers
- ❑ bananas
- ❑ fake fur
- ❑ masking tape
- ❑ paper and pencils
- ❑ boxes of animal crackers
- ❑ paper cups (also used in Treat to Eat)
- ❑ plastic tablecloth
- ❑ water pistols
- ❑ toy plastic monkeys

- ❑ leather shoelaces
- ❑ craft beads
- ❑ craft feathers

Foods & Tableware
- ❑ graham crackers
- ❑ white canned icing
- ❑ chocolate chips
- ❑ orange sherbet
- ❑ pineapple juice
- ❑ drinking straws
- ❑ napkins, plastic knives, and plastic spoons

Party Partings
- ❑ animal-shaped erasers

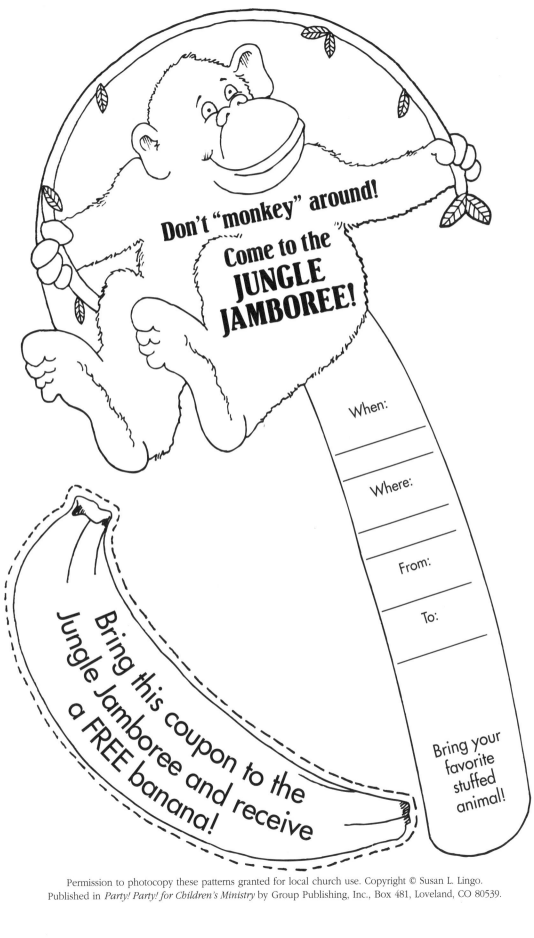

Don't "monkey" around!

Come to the **JUNGLE JAMBOREE!**

When:

Where:

From:

To:

Bring your favorite stuffed animal!

Bring this coupon to the Jungle Jamboree and receive a FREE banana!

The Theme

Snow in summer

Summer Snowball Party

Who says it never snows in July? Cool off with this outdoor celebration during the "dog days" of summer.

PARTY PREPARATIONS

Invitations

● Photocopy the Summer Snowman pattern on page 48 onto stiff paper. Cut out an invitation for each child, and fill in the party information. Mail or hand out the invitations.

For an exciting twist, attach the Summer Snowman invitations to snowball cupcakes, then hand them out!

Decorations

● Scatter foam packing peanuts around the party area. You can also drape fiberfill or quilt batting on the ground and on trees and bushes to give them a "frosty" effect.

● Make an igloo from medium-sized boxes you've spray painted white. Serve snacks from the igloo during the party.

● Cut snowflakes from round coffee filters by folding the filters into thirds, then using scissors to cut designs around the edges. Open the filters, then use fishing line to hang them from trees.

● Hang white and blue crepe paper streamers to add a "chill" to the air. For an extra-festive touch, consider using plastic icicles or tinsel from holiday decorations you have stored at home.

● Stuff a few white plastic trash bags with newspaper to make snowmen. Add construction paper eyes, buttons, mouths, and noses.

GAMES GALORE

Melt Down *(icebreaker)*

As guests arrive, give each of them an ice cube. Challenge kids to learn one another's names before the ice cubes melt! When there's only a puddle of water left, have kids take turns trying to tell everyone's names.

Silly Skiing *(activity)*

Before the party, cut five heavyweight, plastic trash bags along the sides so that they'll open into rectangles. Use duct tape to tape the rectangles end to end to create a long length of plastic. Or purchase a long sheet of heavy landscaping plastic. Lay the "ski slide" on the ground near the party area. When kids are ready to go "silly skiing," pour water down the length of the slide or place a water hose on the slide to create a super slick surface. Position helpers at the ends of the slide to keep it in place, then invite kids to take turns sliding down the plastic. Encourage them to "ski" on their tummies, backs, and knees, but not to run. Add more water as needed.

Snowball Fight *(game)*

Hand children each a large marshmallow "snowball." Tell kids not to eat their snowballs because they'll need them for a fun snowball fight! Form two groups, and designate a center line. Tell kids the object of the game is to toss as many snowballs as possible to the other side of the center line in 30 seconds. Have kids begin tossing their snowballs when you say "snowball!" After the game, hand out fresh marshmallow snowballs to eat. Save the "used" marshmallows for the next game.

Snow Stacking *(game)*

Form two groups, and divvy up the marshmallow "snowballs" used in the last game. Tell kids the object of this game is for each team to cooperatively stack its snowballs into a giant tower. Explain that the first group to stack all of its snowballs into a tower that doesn't fall down gets its choice of snowball cupcakes or miniature foam "snowballs." (White foam balls are available at any craft store in many sizes.) Be sure the rest of the guests get their choice, too!

Snow Sculpting *(game)*

Have kids find partners. Hand each pair a vinyl place mat. Tell kids they'll sculpt snow statues from shaving cream then guess what other pairs have created. Give each pair a tennis ball-sized puff of shaving cream to sculpt. Encourage partners to work quickly since the shaving cream "snow" will melt! After a couple of minutes, let pairs guess what the others have made. Make sure everyone rinses his or her hands well after this game. This is a great activity to use just before treat time—everyone's hands will be as "white as snow."

No-Melt Masterpieces (craft)

Hand each child five miniature foam balls, five large marshmallows, and 10 toothpicks. (Use pretzel sticks if your guests are very young.) Let children create masterpieces by using toothpicks to attach the foam "snowballs" and marshmallows together. Suggest shapes such as snowflakes, snowmen, snow animals, snow cars, or snow spaceships. Let kids take their creations home as party favors.

TREAT TO EAT

Sundae Snow Cups

Set out vanilla ice cream or frozen yogurt and a variety of toppings, such as chocolate, strawberry, or caramel sauces; peanuts; raisins; and tiny candies. Provide paper bowls and plastic spoons for kids to make their own delicious "snowy" sundaes.

PARTY PARTINGS

As kids are leaving, mention that snowballs in July might seem impossible, but that we know all things are possible with God! Express your delight at seeing them, and hand each child a white pingpong ball "snowball" with these words written in permanent marker on it: "God Can Do Anything!"

SHOPPING LIST
FOR SUMMER SNOWBALL PARTY

Invitations
- [ ] envelopes and stamps

Decorations
- [ ] foam packing peanuts
- [ ] white spray paint
- [ ] medium-sized boxes
- [ ] round coffee filters
- [ ] white and blue crepe paper
- [ ] white plastic trash bags
- [ ] newspaper

- [ ] construction paper

Games & Activities
- [ ] ice cubes
- [ ] heavyweight plastic trash bags
- [ ] duct tape
- [ ] large marshmallows
- [ ] snowball cupcakes
- [ ] miniature foam balls
- [ ] vinyl place mats
- [ ] shaving cream
- [ ] toothpicks

Foods & Tableware
- [ ] vanilla ice cream
- [ ] chocolate, strawberry, or caramel ice cream sauces
- [ ] peanuts, raisins, tiny candies
- [ ] napkins, paper bowls, and plastic spoons

Party Partings
- [ ] white pingpong balls
- [ ] permanent fine-tipped marker

Summer SNOWBALL Party!

Come cool off with some frosty fun!

When: _____

Where: _____

From: _____ To: _____

Wear a swimsuit or old clothes— and bring your favorite beach towel!

Outta This World Party

The Theme

A trip to the stars

When you blast off for fantastic fun with this exciting party, your kids will go into orbit!

PARTY PREPARATIONS

Invitations

● Photocopy the Rocket Ship pattern on page 52 onto stiff paper. Cut out the patterns and each porthole. Fill in the party information. Color and decorate the front of the rocket ship with markers and self-adhesive star stickers. You may wish to toss a bit of shiny star-shaped confetti in the envelope along with the invitation. Mail or hand out the invitations.

For a different kind of invitation, blow up long balloons and write the party information on the balloons with permanent markers. Then deflate the balloons and send them to your guests.

Decorations

● Make a grand entryway by attaching small Christmas tree lights around the door frame. Twinkling lights provide a breathtaking effect!

● Consider covering the walls and/or the ceiling with black landscaping plastic or black trash bags.

● Color balloons to look like moons, planets, and the earth, and use fishing line to hang the balloons from the ceiling.

● Cut star shapes out of poster board, then use glitter to make them sparkle. Use fishing line to suspend the stars from the ceiling.

● Roll poster board into large tubes, then decorate them to look like rocket ships. Set the rocket ships on aluminum pie plates or tin cans. For super special effects, put small pieces of dry ice in the aluminum pie plates to create a "ready-to-blast-off" look! (You can find dry ice at most ice companies. Be sure not to handle it without gloves! Ask the salesperson for details.)

GAMES GALORE

Space Partners *(icebreaker)*

Set out poster board, tape, markers, construction paper, and self-adhesive star stickers. As kids arrive, have them find partners and work together to create their own rocket ships. When the rocket ships are finished, have kids "fly" around the room to meet the other "astronauts."

Gravity Walk *(game)*

Before this game, glue felt to the bottoms of four bricks. You'll also need two pairs of shoelaces. Form two groups, and have them get in lines at one end of the party area. Tie bricks on the feet of the first person in each line. Tell kids their mission is to walk to the other end of the room in their "gravity boots," touch the wall, and return to their group so the next "astronaut" can go. Explain that it's important to walk—not run—because you don't want any astronauts with broken toes! The first group to complete its "space walk" gets its choice of outer space stickers. Be sure everyone gets a sticker.

Pass the Planets *(game)*

Blow up four balloons and tie them off. Have kids sit in a circle on the floor. Hand the balloon "planets" to four different children. Two of the kids will pass their planets in one direction while the other two will pass their planets in the opposite direction. Tell kids you're the Space Commander and will give them orders such as "Speed up," "Slow down," or "Reverse direction." If anyone is caught with two planets at one time, he or she becomes the next Space Commander. Continue playing until every guest has had a chance to be the Space Commander. Hand out gumball "planets" to every player for prizes.

Lunar Rock Hunt *(game)*

Before the party, spray paint medium-sized rocks with silver or gold spray paint. Allow the rocks to dry thoroughly. Before the party, hide the "lunar rocks." Hand each child a paper lunch sack. Tell kids they have one minute to collect as many lunar rocks as they can. Let kids keep the lunar rocks they find as unusual party favors.

Moonscapes *(craft)*

Before the party, stir a few tablespoonsful of glitter into a small pail of sand. Set out the glittery sand, black markers, foam meat trays, white craft glue, and outer space stickers. Let kids color the top halves of the foam trays with black markers. Have them spread glue along the bottom halves of the foam trays, then sprinkle glittery sand on the glue. Let them choose stickers to put in the "sky."

TREAT TO EAT

Satellites 'n' Rockets

Set out cheese cubes, grapes, pineapple chunks, marshmallows, and pretzel sticks. Let kids make satellites and rocket ships by skewering the cheese cubes and fruit onto pretzel sticks.

Pluto Punch

Mix fruit punch with lemon-lime soda. Serve in clear plastic cups.

For an unusual treat, offer kids "astronaut ice cream." This unusual freeze-dried treat is eaten by NASA astronauts and is available at many science centers and learning toy shops. Or contact: American Outdoor Products, 800-253-8283.

PARTY PARTINGS

Gather kids and mention that when we feel really good, we say we're feeling "outta this world!" Point out that there's no better feeling than following Jesus and that's why we want to tell everyone about him. Hand children each a sheet of self-adhesive star stickers to remind them that following Jesus is "outta this world!"

SHOPPING LIST
FOR OUTTA THIS WORLD PARTY

Invitations
- [ ] self-adhesive star stickers (also used in Games Galore and in Party Partings)
- [ ] envelopes and stamps

Decorations
- [ ] small Christmas tree lights
- [ ] balloons (also used in Games Galore)
- [ ] fishing line
- [ ] poster board (also used in Games Galore)

- [ ] glitter (also used in Games Galore)
- [ ] aluminum pie plates

Games & Activities
- [ ] construction paper
- [ ] felt
- [ ] four bricks
- [ ] two pairs of shoelaces
- [ ] outer space stickers that include planets, spaceships, and stars
- [ ] gumballs
- [ ] medium-sized rocks

- [ ] gold or silver metallic spray paint
- [ ] paper lunch sacks
- [ ] sand
- [ ] black markers
- [ ] foam meat trays

Foods & Tableware
- [ ] cheese cubes
- [ ] grapes
- [ ] pineapple chunks
- [ ] marshmallows
- [ ] pretzel sticks
- [ ] fruit punch
- [ ] lemon-lime soda
- [ ] napkins and clear plastic cups

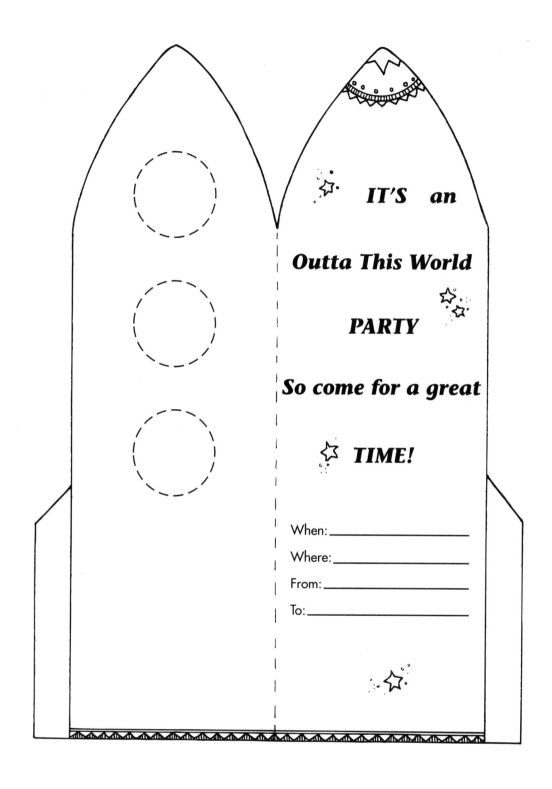

IT'S an

Outta This World

PARTY

So come for a great

TIME!

When: _____

Where: _____

From: _____

To: _____

Kickoff Celebration

The Theme

Starting a new year

This party is a great way to kick off a new year and bond your kids into a "winning team"!

PARTY PREPARATIONS

Invitations

● Photocopy the Soccer Ball pattern on page 56 onto stiff paper. Cut out a party invitation for each child, and fill in the party information. Mail or hand out the invitations.

For unforgettable invitations, purchase inexpensive 4-inch rubber balls at any discount center, and use a permanent marker to write the party information directly on the rubber balls. "Bounce" the party invitations to your kids and watch 'em smile! (Be sure to include information about bringing a new white T-shirt to decorate.)

Decorations

● Turn your doorway into a goal post by stringing crepe paper down both sides of the door frame and across the center.

● Display team pennants and pompons around your party area. Check with church members to see if anyone has team paraphernalia for you to borrow. You may also make simple pennants by taping construction paper triangles to drinking straws.

● Scatter a variety of sports equipment around the party area. You might include basketballs, baseballs and bats, baseball hats, soccer balls, tennis balls, bowling balls, volleyballs, and a hockey stick or surfboard. Mention to the guests that these are party decorations only!

● Use colored vinyl tape from a hardware store to make a 5-foot square on the floor. Be sure each side of the square is a different color. You'll use this colorful square during the party.

● If you have access to a referee's shirt, wear it! It makes a novel party outfit and will designate you as the Party Ref!

GAMES GALORE

Sports Stars *(icebreaker)*

Before the party, photocopy the Sports Star Card patterns on page 57 onto stiff paper. You'll need a Sports Star Card for each guest.

Set out tape, glue sticks, and scissors. As guests arrive, take their photographs with an instant-print camera. Hand kids each a Sports Star Card, a sheet of paper, and a pencil. When the pictures are developed, have kids cut out their photographs and glue them over the faces on their sports cards. Let kids work together to tape the sports cards to their backs, then have kids collect autographs from each "sports star" at the party as they learn one another's names.

Loco Logos *(craft)*

Have kids form pairs. Give each pair paper and a few markers. Challenge each pair to design a team logo for the entire group. (If your group doesn't have a name, begin this activity by brainstorming and voting on a group name.) Encourage kids to keep their logo designs simple and colorful. After five minutes, have kids share their creations, then let kids vote on which logo they'd like to adopt for the year. Let each child trace the logo onto a new sheet of paper, then color the logo with colorful fabric crayons. (Keep in mind that words will transfer in reverse.) Help kids iron the logos on the white T-shirts they've brought according to the directions on the package of fabric crayons. Encourage kids to wear their new "team" shirts to the next class meeting.

Color Code Dodge Ball *(game)*

Have kids form four groups and line up along the sides of the colorful square you taped on the floor. Tell kids this is a goofy game of Dodge Ball. Explain that they'll toss a foam ball back and forth trying to tag opponents on other color lines. Have kids who are tagged join the lines of the people who tagged them. Play until everyone is on one color line.

Partner-Pulley Tag *(game)*

Before the party, cut one 12-inch crepe paper streamer for each pair of kids. Have kids form pairs, then give each pair a paper streamer. Tell pairs to fasten their paper streamers to one partner's back with tape or by tucking it into a belt or waistband. Then have partners lock elbows on one side. Tell kids the object of the game is to snatch other pairs' streamers. If a streamer is snatched, that pair must lock elbows with the pair who snatched the streamer, then reattach the streamer. If two pairs are joined and one of their streamers is snatched, all four kids join the other pair! Play until everyone is joined together.

Cooperative Team Banner *(activity)*

Roll out a 6-foot length of white shelf paper and tape the corners to the floor. Set out markers and crayons. Let kids work together to create a banner for your class. When the banner is finished, display it each time your class meets to remind them what a great "team" they make!

TREAT TO EAT

Ballpark Franks 'n' Chips

Serve hot dogs with all the fixings, including ketchup, mustard, relish, and chopped onions. Set out a basket of chips to go with the "dogs."

Home Run Punch

Serve chilled apple juice with marshmallow "baseballs."

PARTY PARTINGS

Photocopy the Blue Ribbon Award patterns on page 56 onto stiff paper. Cut out an award for each guest. Fold, then tape or glue a 10-inch length of wide blue ribbon to the bottom of the awards. As kids are leaving, point out that being on Jesus' team is the best and that with Jesus as their captain, they're all winners! Hand each child a blue ribbon, and remind kids to wear their "team" T-shirts to the next class meeting.

SHOPPING LIST
FOR KICKOFF CELEBRATION

Invitations
- [ ] envelopes and stamps

Decorations
- [ ] crepe paper (also used in Games Galore)
- [ ] team pennants and pompons
- [ ] sports equipment
- [ ] colored vinyl tape

Games & Activities
- [ ] instant-print camera
- [ ] paper, pencils, and markers
- [ ] fabric crayons
- [ ] iron
- [ ] white T-shirts
- [ ] foam ball
- [ ] white shelf paper
- [ ] crayons

Foods & Tableware
- [ ] hot dogs and buns
- [ ] hot dog toppings
- [ ] basket
- [ ] chips
- [ ] apple juice
- [ ] marshmallows
- [ ] napkins, paper cups, and paper plates

Party Partings
- [ ] wide blue ribbon

SPORTS STAR

Holds the world record for most bananas peeled in five minutes!

SPORTS STAR

SPORTS STAR

Holds the indoor record for the most cereal eaten in one month!

Cereal

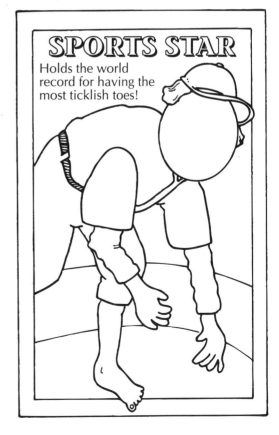

SPORTS STAR

Holds the world record for having the most ticklish toes!

Purple Party

The Theme

The color purple

What party chases away winter blues and puts you in the pink? A purple party!

PARTY PREPARATIONS

Invitations

● Photocopy the Purpledy Grapes pattern on page 61 onto purple paper. Fill in the party information, then add packages of grape soft drink mix to the envelopes to get kids in the mood to "party with purple"! Mail or hand out the invitations.

Decorations

● Make a grape arbor by hanging clusters of artificial or paper grapes around door ways and windows. Be sure to use purple grapes!

● Hang clusters of purple balloons around the party area. Add purple crepe paper streamers for a festive touch.

● Be sure to wear your "best" purple party clothes. A purple T-shirt is an inexpensive party shirt. You may wish to paint the words "Party Purple!" on your T-shirt with glittery fabric paints.

● Check your hardware store for purple light bulbs. They look great in ceiling lights and add a "purpledy" glow to your festivities.

GAMES GALORE

Purpledy Pals *(icebreaker)*

Set out water, purple paint (tempera, acrylic, or watercolor), and small paintbrushes for face painting fun. As your guests arrive, have them each paint a small purple shape on someone else's face or hand. Suggest shapes such as flowers, stars, balloons, hearts, or animals. Challenge kids to collect paint shapes from everyone at the party—and to learn one another's names as they're painting. Assure kids that the paint will wash off with a little soap and water after the party!

The Great Grape Stomp *(game)*

Before the party, half-fill purple balloons with water and tie them off. (Half-filled water balloons are much harder to pop than full ones!) You'll need one water balloon for each child.

Plan to play this game outside or on a large concrete or tile floor. (If you play the game inside, you'll need a mop for cleanup.) Spread a plastic table-cloth, dropcloth, or shower curtain on your playing area. Form two groups, and have them line up on opposite sides of the plastic. Hand each child a purple water balloon. Ask kids to remove their shoes for some splish-splashy fun.

Explain that in Jesus' time, grapes were pressed or stepped on to make fruit juice and wine to drink. Mention that in this game, they'll race to squish their water balloon "grapes." When you say "go," have the first players from each group *gently* place their balloons on the plastic, stomp their balloons to break them, then tag the next people in their lines. The first group to stomp and squish all its grapes is the winner and may be the first to choose a bunch of grapes to nibble. Be sure everyone gets a bunch of grapes to gobble.

Purple Robe Wrap *(game)*

Before the party, cut an 18-inch purple crepe paper streamer for each child. Hand out the streamers, then tell kids that purple is considered a "royal" color—a color for kings. Point out that Jesus is the King of all heaven and earth and that purple is often associated with Jesus. Explain that the object of this game is for the whole group to tie its streamers together, and then wrap the long purple streamer "robe" around the whole group before one minute is up. Encourage kids to cooperate, and be sure everyone gets wrapped up. Point out how Jesus wraps us in his love just as they're wrapped in the purple robe. Drape the long streamer around the room, then hand each child a purple pencil or eraser to remind them that Jesus is King!

Grape Volleyball *(game)*

Play a wacky game of volleyball using a grape as a *really* miniature ball! Use masking tape to mark a center line, then form two groups and have them stand on either side of the center line. Play just like volleyball, but caution kids to volley the "ball" gently. (Be sure to have backup grapes on hand!) Continue playing until one side has 5 points. Have groups switch sides and play once more. If each group wins a game, go into a tiebreaker!

Lively Laces *(craft)*

Let kids create crazy purple shoelaces to wear in their shoes or as ponytail ties or to use as Bible bookmarks. Cover a table with newspaper. Provide a pair of 24- or 36-inch shoelaces for each guest. Set out purple, orange, pink, violet, and black markers, and allow kids to color their shoelaces however they choose. Let kids display or model their finished creations. Encourage everyone to clap after each "work of art" is displayed.

TREAT TO EAT

Crunchy Peanut Butter 'n' Jelly Sandwiches

Set out potato chips, plastic knives, bread, peanut butter, and a jar of grape jelly. Let kids make their own sandwiches. Encourage them to try adding potato chips in the middle for an extra-special taste treat!

Purple Cow Juice

Stir an envelope of presweetened grape soft drink mix into a gallon of milk. Serve the "purple moo juice" in clear plastic cups or paper cups decorated with black "cow spots."

PARTY PARTINGS

Gather kids at the close of the party, and remind them that purple is the royal color that reminds us of Jesus. Hand each child a square of purple craft felt. Encourage kids to take the felt squares home and lay them on their pillows or hang them in their rooms as reminders that Jesus is always the king of their lives.

SHOPPING LIST FOR PURPLE PARTY

Invitations
- ❏ packages of grape soft drink mix
- ❏ envelopes and stamps

Decorations
- ❏ artificial or paper grapes
- ❏ purple balloons
- ❏ purple crepe paper (also used in Games Galore)
- ❏ purple T-shirt

Games & Activities
- ❏ purple paint
- ❏ small paintbrushes
- ❏ plastic tablecloth
- ❏ grapes (lots!)
- ❏ purple pencils
- ❏ masking tape
- ❏ newspaper
- ❏ pairs of 24- or 36-inch shoelaces
- ❏ purple, orange, pink, violet, and black markers

Foods & Tableware
- ❏ potato chips
- ❏ bread
- ❏ peanut butter
- ❏ grape jelly
- ❏ presweetened grape soft drink mix
- ❏ milk
- ❏ napkins, clear plastic cups, and plastic knives

Party Partings
- ❏ purple craft felt

GREAT GRAPES!!

It's a purple party!

When:_____
_____

Where:_____
_____

From:_____

To:_____

Wear
something
purple!

Christmas in July?

The Theme
Christmas celebration

Christmas in December or July? It doesn't matter—after all, isn't Christmas supposed to last all year long?

PARTY PREPARATIONS

Invitations

● Photocopy the Star pattern on page 66 onto yellow paper. Fill in the party information. You may wish to include star or snowflake confetti in the envelope along with the invitation. Mail or hand out the invitations.

For extra-special party invitations, you can make snowflakes by folding round coffee filters into thirds, then cutting designs around the edges. Fill in the party information using a ballpoint pen so the ink won't run on the coffee filter.

Decorations

● Make large, poster-board candy canes to decorate your party area. Tie bright red ribbons around the "necks" of the candy canes.

● String oodles of Christmas tree lights around the party area to give it a real holiday glow. Even if you're hosting a Christmas in July? party outside, be sure to hang Christmas tree lights on bushes or trees around the party area.

● Unpack your Christmas tree decorations and an artificial Christmas tree, or choose a tree outside to decorate. String lights around the tree, but let kids do the rest of the decorating as they arrive! (A large paper tree works well, too.)

● Hang glittery garlands and tinsel around the party area.

● Cut apart brown paper grocery sacks. Make a "manger" by using the brown paper to cover an empty, medium-sized box. You may wish to hang a glittery star above the manger as an extra touch.

● Hang red, green, and white crepe paper streamers and balloons around the party area.

GAMES GALORE

Deck the Halls *(icebreaker)*

Set out a box of Christmas decorations including ornaments for the Christmas tree. As kids arrive, have them form Decorating Duos. Encourage them to work with other Decorating Duos to trim the Christmas tree as they share favorite Christmas memories. Be sure to remind kids that *Jesus* is the reason for the Christmas season!

Star Tag *(game)*

Before the party, cut equal numbers of yellow, blue, and red stars from construction paper. Make sure there's a star for every guest.

Set the manger in the center of the party area, and have kids sit in a large circle around it. Have kids number off by three. Hand each child a colored star, then choose one person from each color group to be Star Taggers. Tell kids you'll call out a number. All players with that number will hop up and try to put their stars in the manger without getting tagged by the Star Taggers. If players are tagged, they go back to the circle with their stars. Warn the Star Taggers not to tag players in their own color group! After you've called each number, count the stars in the manger to see which color group delivered the most stars. Play a few more times with new Star Taggers, then hand each player a star-shaped cookie to enjoy.

Popping With Joy *(activity)*

Before the party, write numbers on small slips of paper, one number for each guest. Put the slips into balloons, then blow up the balloons and tie them off. Wrap small gifts, such as erasers, note pads, combs, or coupons for local hamburger stands or doughnut shops in festive wrapping paper and bows. Place numbered slips of paper on the packages to match the numbered balloons. Place the gifts in the manger just before this activity.

Have kids sit in a circle, then hand each child a balloon. Point out that Christmas is a celebration of love and joy. Tell kids they'll begin passing their balloons around the circle. When you say "stop," have one child begin retelling the story of Jesus' birth beginning with Mary and Joseph's trip to Bethlehem. Continue passing balloons, saying "stop," and letting kids help retell the Christmas story. When you reach the "moment" of Jesus' birth, have kids celebrate the joy by sitting on the balloons they're holding and popping them! Point out that Jesus is a gift of love to us from God. Then let kids find other gifts of joy by matching up the numbers from their balloons with the numbers on the gifts in the manger.

Christmas Stockings *(craft)*

Purchase an inexpensive pair of white tube socks for each guest. (Tube socks fit feet of any size or shape.) Set out fabric paints, and let kids decorate crazy pairs of "Christmas stockings" to wear. Encourage kids to decorate only on one side of each sock and to use Christmas symbols such as stars, hearts, crosses, and the name "Jesus." Use clothespins to clip the socks to wire coat hangers to dry as you enjoy party snacks.

TREAT TO EAT

Fruitcake Jumbles

Set out a plate of graham crackers, canned icing, plastic knives, and bowls of dried fruits, such as raisins, apples, cherries, pears, banana chips, and apricots. You may wish to snip the fruit into small bits using clean scissors. Invite kids to spread icing on their graham crackers then decorate them with dried fruits.

Spiced Apple Cider

Serve chilled apple cider in colorful party cups. For a special touch, use Christmas candy molds to make holiday-shaped ice cubes.

PARTY PARTINGS

As kids gather to leave, hand each child a small pocket mirror tied with a red ribbon. Mention that Jesus is the greatest gift of love and that we can spread that love by giving of ourselves to others. Encourage kids to look in the mirror each day and thank Jesus for the gift of love he's given us.

SHOPPING LIST
FOR CHRISTMAS IN JULY?

Invitations
- [ ] envelopes and stamps

Decorations
- [ ] poster board
- [ ] red ribbon (also used in Party Partings)
- [ ] Christmas tree lights
- [ ] artificial Christmas tree and tree decorations (also used in Games Galore)
- [ ] tinsel and garlands
- [ ] medium-sized box and paper grocery sacks (also used in Games Galore)
- [ ] red, green, and white crepe paper

and balloons (also used in Games & Activities)

Games & Activities
- [ ] Christmas decorations
- [ ] red, blue, and yellow construction paper
- [ ] star-shaped cookies
- [ ] small slips of paper
- [ ] small gifts, such as erasers, note pads, combs, or coupons for hamburgers or doughnuts
- [ ] festive wrapping paper
- [ ] bows
- [ ] white tube socks
- [ ] fabric paints

- [ ] clothespins
- [ ] wire coat hangers

Foods & Tableware
- [ ] graham crackers
- [ ] canned icing
- [ ] dried fruits, such as raisins, apples, cherries, pears, banana chips, and apricots
- [ ] apple cider
- [ ] napkins, paper plate, paper bowls, colorful paper cups, and plastic knives

Party Partings
- [ ] small pocket mirrors

It's
a
Christmas in July Party!
Come and get in the holiday spirit!

When: _____

Where: _____ To: _____

From: _____

The Great Gobbler Get-Together!

Celebrate God's goodness with this zany Thanksgiving party.

PARTY PREPARATIONS

Invitations

● Photocopy the Feathered Turkey pattern on page 71 onto stiff paper. Cut out the tail feathers, then attach them to the turkey shape using a paper fastener so the tail fans out. Fill in the party information. You may wish to include a colorful craft feather in the envelope. Mail or hand out the invitations.

Decorations

● Scatter craft feathers around the party area.

● Hang brown, orange, yellow, and red crepe paper streamers around the party area. Add yellow and orange balloons for an extra-festive touch.

● Make a goofy turkey by cutting apart paper grocery sacks, then using them to cover a medium-sized box. Add construction paper tail feathers, head, comb, feet, and a beak. Use a black marker to draw eyes. You'll use this zany turkey to play a game during the party.

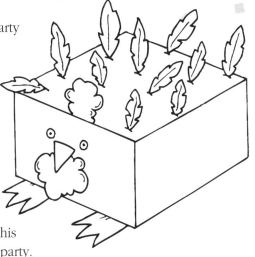

GAMES GALORE

Glitter Critter (icebreaker)

Cover a table with newspaper. Set out markers, glitter glue, craft feathers, and a small stone for each child. As kids arrive, have them work together and share materials as they create "glitter-critter turkeys" by decorating the stones with glitter glue and craft feathers. Encourage kids to use markers to add beaks, eyes, and red gobblers. Set the stones aside to dry.

Pin the Tail on the Turkey (game)

Set the box turkey at one end of the party area. Have kids form two groups and line up at the other end of the room. Hand each child a craft feather. Tell kids the object of the game is to do the "turkey wobbler" across the room, poke their feathers into the turkey, then return to their lines so the next person can go. Have kids practice the turkey wobbler by tucking their thumbs under their arms and squatting on their heels to "walk." When one group gets all of its feathers in the turkey, have that group celebrate by making turkey gobbling sounds. After the relay, let each child choose a craft feather to keep as a prize.

Pass the Turkey, Please! (game)

Have kids form a circle. Hand the box turkey to one child, a potato to a second child, and an apple to a third. Tell kids this game will remind them of all the yummy foods they have at Thanksgiving.

Have players begin passing the items to their right in some unusual way such as over their heads, between their legs, or balanced on their open palms. Each time you say "switch," have the children holding the items change the way they are being passed. Clap slowly to set a rhythmic pace as children pass the items, then gradually increase the speed as the game goes on. If anyone gets caught holding two items at once, have that player gobble like a turkey, then hand one of the items to another player before continuing.

Thankful Wishbones (activity)

Before this game, photocopy the Wishbone pattern on page 72 onto brown construction paper. Cut out a wishbone for each player.

Have kids form pairs. Hand each pair two paper wishbones. Tell kids that this activity will help them think of things they have to be thankful for, such as friends, parents, good food, warm clothes, and safe places to live. Encourage kids to think of something they're especially thankful for, then "break" one of the paper wishbones. Have the partners who are holding the bigger halves tell what they're thankful for, then have the other partners share. Let pairs use their other wishbones to repeat the activity, but this time have partners each think of one reason they're thankful for Jesus. When kids are finished, you may want to let kids tell the entire group their thankful responses.

Cornucopias *(craft)*

Set out brown construction paper, tape, markers, stickers, and bowls of finger foods, such as peanuts in the shell, cereal loops, raisins, miniature marshmallows, and small candies. Let kids decorate one side of their papers then fold and tape their papers into cone-shaped cornucopias with the decorated side out. Invite kids to fill their cornucopias with their choice of the goodies you've set out. Encourage kids to take their cornucopias home and share the goodies as family members take turns telling what they're especially thankful for.

TREAT TO EAT

Feast Fest

Let kids gobble with delight as they work together to create a monster turkey sandwich! Set out a 3-foot loaf of bread (available at submarine sandwich shops) or the longest loaf of French bread you can find. Provide sliced turkey, lettuce, sliced tomatoes, pickles, and sliced cheese. After the turkey sub is made, cut the sandwich into 4-inch sections, and let kids add their own condiments. Set out bowls of corn chips to enjoy with the feast. Be sure to say a prayer of thanksgiving before your feast begins!

Gobbler Juice

Serve orange juice mixed with orange soda.

PARTY PARTINGS

Let kids glue their glitter critters to index cards. Have kids write on their cards, "Thank you, God." Help younger guests write on their cards. Encourage kids to set their glitter critters on the dining table at home to remind them to thank God for all the good things he sends.

SHOPPING LIST
FOR THE GREAT GOBBLER GET-TOGETHER!

Invitations
- ☐ paper fasteners
- ☐ envelopes and stamps

Decorations
- ☐ craft feathers (also used in Games Galore)
- ☐ brown, orange, yellow, and red crepe paper
- ☐ yellow and orange balloons
- ☐ medium-sized box (also used in Games Galore)
- ☐ paper grocery sacks

- ☐ construction paper
- ☐ black marker

Games & Activities
- ☐ newspaper
- ☐ glitter glue
- ☐ small stones
- ☐ one potato
- ☐ one apple
- ☐ brown construction paper
- ☐ stickers
- ☐ finger foods, such as peanuts in the shell, cereal loops, raisins, miniature marshmallows, and small candies

Foods & Tableware
- ☐ 3-foot loaf of bread
- ☐ turkey sandwich meat
- ☐ lettuce, tomatoes, and pickles
- ☐ cheese slices
- ☐ condiments
- ☐ corn chips
- ☐ orange juice
- ☐ orange soda
- ☐ cutting knife
- ☐ napkins, small paper plates, and paper cups

Party Partings
- ☐ index cards

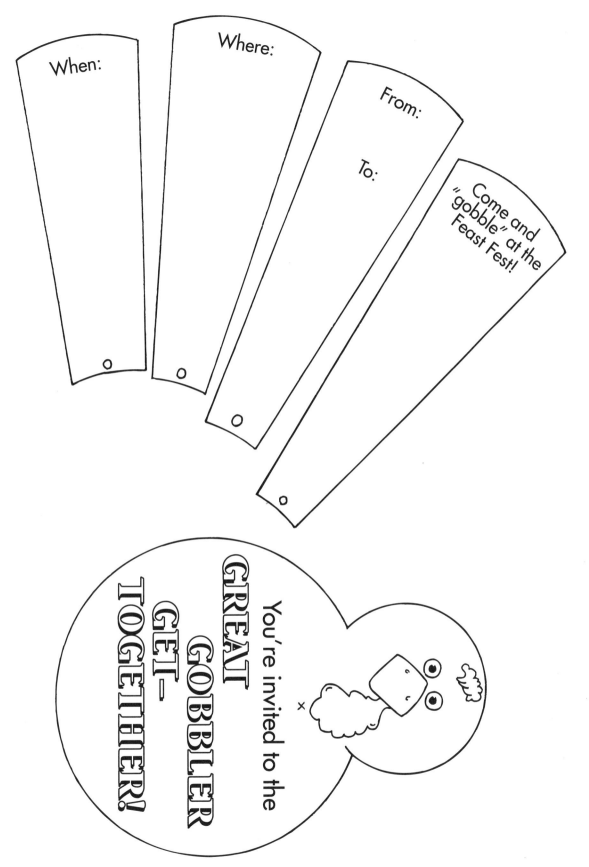

When:

Where:

From:

To:

Come and "gobble" at the Feast Fest!

You're invited to the
GREAT
GOBBLER
GET-
TOGETHER!

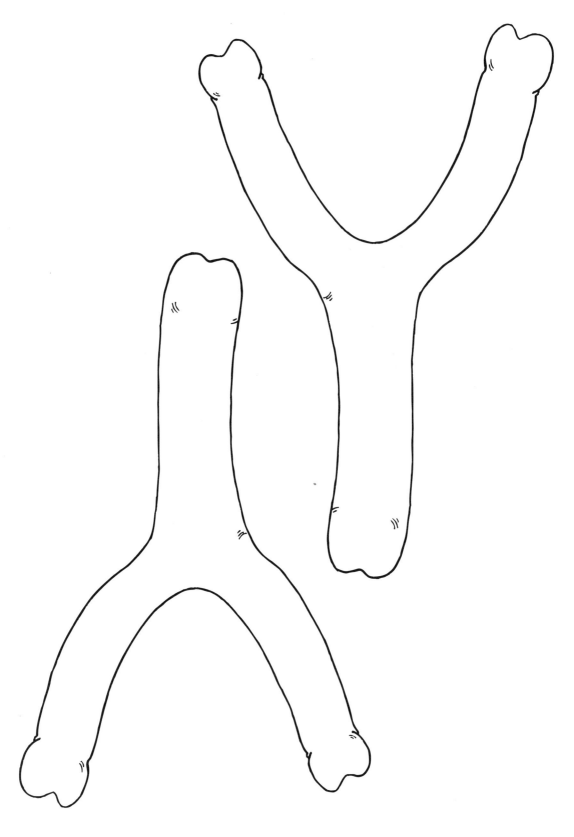

Hoppin' Easter Hoopla

The Theme

Easter

Celebrate the newness of spring as you help kids experience the joy of knowing that Jesus is alive.

PARTY PREPARATIONS

Invitations

● Photocopy the Baby Bird pattern on page 76 onto stiff yellow or blue paper. Fill in the party information, then fold the invitations and place them in colorful, plastic pull-apart eggs. If you're sending invitations by mail, use yellow or blue envelopes instead of the plastic eggs.

Decorations

● Hang lots of pastel-colored crepe paper and balloons for a festive spring-time effect.

● Tape pastel-colored tissue paper over the windows. Sunlight shining through the tissue paper gives the windows a soft, stained glass look.

● Scatter artificial flowers around your party area to create a spring garden effect. Check music stores or the library for CDs or cassette tapes that have nature sounds recorded on them. Playing soft music with the sounds of birds is a great touch!

GAMES GALORE

Eggstra Special Friends *(icebreaker)*

Before your guests arrive, hide colorful plastic or hard-boiled eggs around the party area. Encourage children to team up with one or two other party goers and hunt for eggs. When each team member has an egg, let them decorate their eggs together. Provide colorful permanent markers, glitter glue, confetti, and bits of ribbon to decorate the eggs. Set the eggs in an empty egg carton to dry.

Egg-Toss *(game)*

Hide a small toy chick (or picture of a chick) in a pull-apart egg. Put the egg in a paper sack with other pull-apart eggs, then mix them up. Have kids stand in a large circle. Hand each child a plastic egg. Be sure someone gets the egg with the hidden chick. When you say "egg-toss," have kids begin tossing the eggs back and forth across and around the circle until you say "freeze." Then have kids open the eggs. The player with the chick gets to choose three jelly beans to eat and then takes a seat in the center of the circle.

Remove one egg from play and begin again. Play until there are two children tossing the egg with the chick. Encourage the children in the center to clap and cheer. Be sure everyone gets three jelly beans to eat. Remind kids that the joy of Easter morning was in finding the empty tomb and in knowing that Jesus is alive!

Ol' Fashioned Jelly Bean Hunt *(activity)*

Before this activity, have your helper hide jelly beans around the party area. When the candies are hidden, hand each child a small plastic sandwich bag. Explain that you'll have a jelly bean hunt, but that at the end of the game you'll divide up the treats so everyone will have an equal share. As kids enjoy nibbling their jelly beans, point out that the colors can help us remember important things about the Easter story. Red stands for the blood Jesus shed on the cross for us, white reminds us that Jesus' forgiveness makes us clean, yellow and pink remind us to be joyful because Jesus is alive, and green reminds us of the new life Jesus gives.

Rock and Roll *(game)*

Tape five paper cups in a row, and lay them on the floor so that the open ends face your guests. Form two groups, and have them stand six feet from the "caves." Hand each group a pingpong ball. Let children take turns rolling the "stones" into the caves. Score 1 point each time a stone rolls into a cave. Play until one group reaches 10. Invite the children in that group to choose prizes, such as a special Easter eraser or note pad or pieces of rock candy. Then let the children in the other group choose prizes.

Window Wonders *(craft)*

Purchase clear plastic vinyl at a fabric or discount store. Cut a 12-inch square for each child. Photocopy the "Jesus Is Alive" pattern on page 77. Make a photocopy for each child.

Cover a table with newspaper. Set out the vinyl squares, colorful permanent markers, and the photocopies of the "Jesus Is Alive" pattern. Show kids how to lay a square of vinyl over the pattern, then use the markers to trace and color the design. Have kids rest their hands on sheets of scrap paper so they don't smear parts of the designs they've already colored. Tell kids to be careful not to get marker ink on their clothes. When the projects are finished, stick them on a window and let kids see the beautiful "stained glass" designs. Encourage kids to retell the story of the first Easter. Point out our joy in knowing that Jesus is alive and with us today!

TREAT TO EAT

Praise Cakes

Set out cupcakes, plastic knives, canned icing, and cake decorations, such as green coconut and tiny jelly beans. Let kids each decorate a cupcake to enjoy.

Son-shine Juice

Serve chilled orange-pineapple juice.

PARTY PARTINGS

Before the party, cut three 12-inch crepe paper streamers for each child. As kids leave, hand out the streamers. Encourage kids to wave the streamers with joy and tell everyone that Jesus is alive.

SHOPPING LIST
FOR HOPPIN' EASTER HOOPLA

Invitations
- ❑ plastic pull-apart eggs (also used in Games Galore)
- ❑ envelopes and stamps

Decorations
- ❑ pastel-colored crepe paper (also used in Party Partings)
- ❑ pastel-colored balloons
- ❑ pastel-colored tissue paper
- ❑ artificial flowers

Games & Activities
- ❑ colorful permanent markers
- ❑ glitter glue
- ❑ confetti
- ❑ ribbon
- ❑ empty egg carton
- ❑ small toy chick
- ❑ paper sack
- ❑ jelly beans (two bags)
- ❑ small plastic sandwich bags
- ❑ paper cups (also used in Treat to Eat)
- ❑ pingpong balls
- ❑ small prizes, such as Easter erasers or note pads
- ❑ clear plastic vinyl

Foods & Tableware
- ❑ cupcakes
- ❑ canned icing
- ❑ cake decorations, such as green coconut and tiny jelly beans
- ❑ orange-pineapple juice
- ❑ napkins and plastic knives

It's a

Hoppin'
Easter Hoopla . . .

and you're invited!

When: _____

Where: _____

From: _____ To: _____

Celebration of Love

Have a heart—and a whole lot of fun—with a Valentine's Day celebration of love that spreads!

PARTY PREPARATIONS

Invitations

● Photocopy the Heart pattern on page 81 onto red or pink construction paper. Cut out an invitation for each child. Tape red and white crepe paper or ribbon streamers to the bottoms of the invitations. You may wish to include a few candy hearts in the envelopes. Mail or hand out invitations.

Decorations

● Make a large heart in your doorway with crepe paper. As kids step through the heart, point out that the only way to God is *through* Jesus' love!

● Hang red, white, and pink crepe paper streamers around the party area for a festive touch.

● Toss red, white, and pink balloons around your party area. You may wish to use special Valentine's balloons available at most party stores.

● Scatter red and white confetti on party tables.

● Cut a large heart from red poster board and on it write, "We love Jesus!" Tape the heart to a wall, and set out pink and red crayons nearby. As kids arrive, encourage them to sign the party heart to show that they love Jesus too!

GAMES GALORE

Human Valentine Cards *(icebreaker)*

Set out tape, a few markers, and a box or two of inexpensive valentines. As kids arrive, invite them to sign a card for each person at the party. Then let kids go around and tape cards to the other guests and learn their names. Challenge kids to see how many cards they can collect on their clothes and how many names they're able to remember!

Pass the Love *(game)*

Form two groups, and have each group form a line. Give each child a plastic spoon. Place paper cups in front of the first players in line, and hand the last players in each line 10 candy hearts. Tell kids the object of the game is to use the plastic spoons to pass the candy hearts to the front of the line. When a heart reaches the first person in line, that person will drop the heart in the paper cup. The first group to collect all its candy hearts in its paper cup gets to choose a box of candy hearts as a prize. Be sure the kids in the other group each receive a box of hearts, too.

Snatch the Heart *(game)*

Before the party, cut a 6-inch paper heart from red poster board. If you have an empty, heart-shaped candy box, use it instead.

Place the heart on the floor in the center of the room. Have kids form a large circle around the heart, then number off by fours. Tell kids that when you call out a number, all the kids with that number should try to snatch the heart and return to the circle before being tagged by one of the other players. If a player is tagged, everyone returns to the circle and a new number is called. If someone successfully snatches the heart, he or she can choose one candy heart to keep. The player with the most hearts collected in 10 rounds gets his or her pick of a heart-shaped pencil or eraser. Then let all the other kids choose a prize.

Sweet Charades *(activity)*

Set out a bowl of candy "conversation" hearts. Let pairs of kids take turns choosing a heart and acting out the phrase written on it. For a fun twist with older kids, let each pair choose 10 hearts and see who can make the longest conversation. Allow pairs to read their goofy sentences aloud.

Heart Sculptures *(craft)*

Before the party, purchase various heart-shaped items at a craft store, such as wooden cutouts, small buttons, and tiny erasers. You'll also need to purchase self-hardening clay.

Cover a table with newspaper, then set out the hearts. Hand each child a golf ball-sized lump of clay and a square of aluminum foil. Show kids how to flatten the clay on the foil using the palms of their hands. Then let kids press different-sized heart shapes into the clay. Explain that the clay will air-dry in a few days. Then they can use their creations as paperweights to remind them that love comes in many shapes and sizes—but that Jesus' love is always the same!

TREAT TO EAT

Edible Valentines

Set out napkins, plastic knives, heart-shaped sugar cookies, pink canned icing, and tiny cinnamon candies. Invite kids to create their own edible valentines by spreading icing on the cookies and decorating them with cinnamon candies.

Cinnamon Spice Punch

Mix apple juice, cinnamon, and lemon-lime soda in a punch bowl. Chill the party punch with plenty of ice cubes. For a festive touch, use heart-shaped candy molds to make red ice cubes to float in the punch!

PARTY PARTINGS

As each child is leaving, spread a bit of love by offering each departing guest a warm hug or handshake. Be sure to remind them that Jesus loves them all yearlong—not just on Valentine's Day. Let kids each choose a party streamer and balloon to take home.

SHOPPING LIST
FOR CELEBRATION OF LOVE

Invitations
- [ ] red and white crepe paper (also used in Decorations)
- [ ] envelopes and stamps

Decorations
- [ ] pink crepe paper
- [ ] red, white, and pink balloons
- [ ] red and white confetti
- [ ] red poster board (also used in Games Galore)
- [ ] pink and red crayons

Games & Activities
- [ ] two boxes of inexpensive valentines
- [ ] plastic spoons
- [ ] paper cups (also used in Treat to Eat)
- [ ] candy hearts (lots!)
- [ ] heart-shaped pencils and erasers
- [ ] heart-shaped craft items
- [ ] self-hardening clay
- [ ] newspaper

- [ ] aluminum foil

Foods & Tableware
- [ ] heart-shaped sugar cookies
- [ ] pink canned icing
- [ ] tiny cinnamon candies
- [ ] apple juice
- [ ] cinnamon
- [ ] lemon-lime soda
- [ ] punch bowl
- [ ] napkins and plastic knives

You're invited to a

Celebration of Love!

When: _____

Where: _____

From: _____ To: _____

Carnivals and Special Events

Introduction to Carnivals and Special Events

How can you reach a lot of kids at one time with the great news about Jesus? Have a kid-carnival! A church-sponsored carnival or special event can be a joyous outreach into the community and can impact great numbers of children and their parents. Yet many churches shy away from offering carnivals and other special events. Why? Often because of the following three "monster myths."

Church carnivals require too much preparation.

#1

Don't be put off by "preparation dread." While it's true that large special events require more time and thought than parties for smaller numbers, the planning strategies for both are remarkably similar. If you can manage the pesky details, many of your planning headaches disappear! The carnivals presented in *Party! Party!* are designed to remove the roadblocks that may draw you away from your carnival goal—bringing kids to Christ.

Church carnivals don't have to be elaborately staged productions. For example, the Great Cookie Carnival requires just one week to pull together—yet offers kids the same Christ-centered celebration of love as carnivals which require a month or more of preparation! In the pages that follow, you'll find carnivals that work for every church.

Church carnivals cost too much.

#2

Decidedly untrue! You can invest as much or as little as your church budget allows and still offer kids a quality event. With a few creative, willing volunteers and a handful of supplies such as markers, crepe paper, and tape, you can set the stage for wonderful events at a fraction of what many churches spend. Most activities and games require only basic booths constructed from tables, benches, or large boxes draped with brightly colored paper or fabric tablecloths for a festive touch. Then add a splash of excitement with clever signs, and you've created an exciting, eye-catching carnival midway that's sure to be inviting to any child—and most adults, too! The carnivals included in *Party! Party!* offer any church—regardless of size or finances—the opportunity to reach out into the community with Jesus' love.

Church carnivals don't make a real difference— they're just a fun time for kids.

#**3**

Don't let this familiar rationalization keep you from planning a carnival outreach. Carnivals *are* a fun time for kids—and they *do* make a difference! Many children who don't normally attend Sunday school or church will come to a neighborhood or community church carnival "just for fun"—and it may be the only opportunity they'll have to learn about Jesus! If even *one* child is touched by your special event, isn't the time, cost, preparation, and *fun* more than worth it? Jesus himself said, "The harvest is plentiful but the workers are few" (Matthew 9:37, New International Version). Church carnivals are wonderful tools in those plentiful fields of harvest!

KEYS TO SUCCESS

All right, so you just have to manage the pesky details, gather a few colorful booths, and you're ready for fun? Almost. But first you need the following three keys to unlock the secrets of successful special events.

1 Planning

Solid, organized planning will significantly cut your preparation time. That's why it's vital to choose a leader. One person coordinating the carnival's organization, checklists, and helpers can keep plans focused and on track. The leader's two main functions are organization and delegation. Leaders recruit carnival helpers, assign helpers to booths or specific activities, and keep track of the organizational checklists which are provided in this book. It may help you to picture the planning roles as something similar to a family tree.

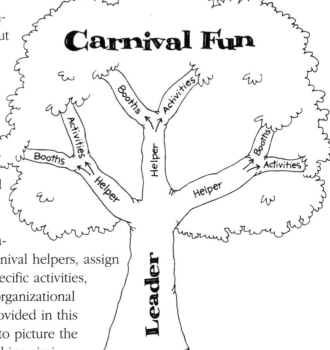

It's essential for the carnival leader or chairperson to hold an initial planning meeting with helpers who will be involved in the event. Use this meeting to assign specific booths to helpers, decide on the foods you may wish to sell (to help defray carnival costs!), plan general decorations, and decide what prizes or treats you'd like to give children at each booth. A planning meeting is the backbone of your special event and will get everyone started on the same path.

As preparation goes forward, the carnival leader needs to stay in close contact with the helpers to be sure they're pulling things together on schedule. This way the workload is evenly distributed and everyone takes equal responsibility for making the special event a success.

A crucial part of planning involves announcing and advertising your special event. The public needs to know about the great things you're planning! Posting fliers at local stores and businesses around town really gets the word out. Placing fliers on doorknobs and car windshields is another great way to spread the news. Use the photocopiable flier on page 90 to announce your event in style. Or use the photocopiable announcements included with each of the three carnival ideas that follow. Simply photocopy the appropriate flier, tack it up or enlarge it, and add color. An especially creative "PR" person could use the pattern to create a giant banner to post in your church's front yard!

If you plan to use the media to announce your special event, you may want to use the Media Release on page 96. Simply photocopy the form and fill in your event information. Then ask local radio stations and newspapers to include the news release in their community announcements a week prior to your event.

The next step in preparing a successful event is to gather supplies. The checklists on pages 92–95 will keep you thoroughly organized and take care of even the smallest planning detail! Keep all the forms in a special folder for quick, easy reference when you need to touch base with helpers or make sure a particular job has been done. The following tips will help you use each form effectively.

● **The Leader Ledger:** Use this form to outline your special event and to record your helpers' names and phone numbers. Also use this form to keep a record of which helpers are in charge of each activity.

● **The Carnival Countdown:** This invaluable checklist breaks planning into specific stages for the carnival leader. From the initial planning meeting to the moment your first guests arrive, the Carnival Countdown form will keep your mind clear and focused on the event. Simply check off each item as it's finished and voilà— you're ready to reach kids!

● **Helper's Checklist:** Photocopy this form for each person attending your initial planning meeting. Slide the forms into colorful folders along with bright pencils for note-taking. In this book, you'll find photocopiable pages for each activity booth with setup directions and necessary supplies listed. Simply photocopy these pages and hand them to the appropriate helpers. It's that simple!

● **General Supplies:** There are items needed at every carnival that aren't part of the activity or food booths. Use this shopping list to record what supplies are needed for your particular event. You may want to shop for supplies and take charge of decorating the general area yourself, or you may want to delegate this responsibility.

● **Reimbursement Form:** Photocopy this half-page form, and give a copy to each of your helpers. It's best to give each helper a budget guideline to work within, then have that helper use the form to keep track of his or her expenses. When booths are done and all supplies have been purchased, helpers simply turn the forms into the carnival leader.

2 Recruiting Help

Sometimes the greatest obstacle in planning special events is recruiting helpers. Jump-start your recruiting efforts by announcing the upcoming special event during a church service. Hand out colorful balloons with the following Scripture verse attached: "The harvest is plentiful but the workers are few" (Matthew 9:37, NIV). Explain your vision for reaching into the community with a special event for children. Then circulate a helper sign-up sheet and assure church members that the work will be minimal, the fun unlimited, and that they'll be ministering to many children who might not otherwise hear the message of Jesus' love.

Obviously, the more helpers you muster, the smoother your special event will run. Remember this rule of thumb for the best number of helpers:

> One to five, your event may dive;
> Six to 10, say "amen";
> Seven to 20, *now* you've plenty!

Don't overlook or underestimate the value of teenagers in helping make your special event a real success! Junior and senior high schoolers can be invaluable in decorating the area, assembling and setting up booths, and helping with young guests. Ask your youth pastor if he or she knows of teens who might enjoy participating in a fun, energetic day of ministry!

The carnivals and special events included in *Party! Party!* are unique in their organization and presentation—and they're especially "helper friendly." Each activity comes on it's own photocopiable page with clear instructions for assembling the activity, an illustration of what the finished booth will look like, and directions for running the activity. Each helper will be assigned an activity (game, craft ideas, or food booth) and will be responsible for assembling and running that booth. Simply photocopy the activity pages for the special event you've chosen, then hand the appropriate page to each helper. Your crew will appreciate the simple, clear directions. They'll be enthusiastic about helping with this event *and* the special events you plan in the future!

One final suggestion—consider holding a "Carnival Capers Work Day." Invite all your helpers to come to church one Saturday and bring all their assembly supplies. Provide extra tape, markers, scissors, poster board, crepe paper, glue, construction paper, and white shelf paper. And don't forget juice, coffee, tea, doughnuts—and a camera! Roll up your sleeves, and invite everyone to work on preparing their booths as they enjoy great food, fun, and fellowship!

3 Follow-up

Following up with the children who attend your special event is crucial. Families who don't have a regular church home often join the church that has warmly welcomed them to a carnival or special event! When you extend a warm hand of welcome, then follow up with an "I care about you" note, you're demonstrating Jesus' love in tangible ways people in your community will appreciate. You'll want to make a point of promptly sending thank you notes to guests who attended your event along with an invitation to visit your church. Be sure to use the Welcome Roster on page 98 at the entrance to your event, so you'll have names and addresses of all your guests at your fingertips.

For prompt, friendly, hassle-free follow-up, use the photocopiable thank you note on page 99. You may want to include the Welcome to Our Church! form on page 97. Or place the Welcome to Our Church! form on a sign-in table at the entrance to your event.

Relax. Be creative. And take joy in the fact that you're providing a wonderful community outreach in Jesus' name. Church carnivals and special events may just turn into your church's own special trademark! These hints and tips will help smooth the way for your joyous day of ministry.

● Offer games and activities for a wide age range. Older kids enjoy skill games such as beanbag tosses and Ring-the-Bottle. Young children prefer games of chance, such as picking a toy duck from a water tub to reveal their "prizes."

● Kids love prizes and doodads! But be sure each guest receives a goodie at every booth. Consider these suggestions for prizes: stickers, boxes of raisins or peanuts, combs, pencils, balloons, ribbons, erasers, shiny pennies, individually wrapped candies, whistles, small toys, plastic rings, note pads, barrettes, Scripture cards, bookmarks, buttons, toothbrushes, refrigerator magnets, bubbles, small inspirational posters, and coupons for doughnuts or hamburgers at local stores.

● Always offer a craft table. Allow kids to make one or two inexpensive craft items to take home as reminders of their special time with you.

● Selling food items can help defray carnival costs. But be sure to price foods very inexpensively. Plan to reduce costs rather than cover them entirely.

● If you're on a tight budget, choose a few inexpensive activities. Face painting, initialing rocks with paint pens, twisting balloon animals, and sculpting modeling dough offer great low-cost fun!

● Always keep a first-aid kit ready for minor mishaps.

● Prepare a "first-aid box" for booth repair. Duct tape, scissors, and markers can take care of accidental damage quickly and easily.

● Take pictures during your event. Display the photographs in your church where everyone can enjoy them. This bit of "PR" may help spur on new volunteers in years to come!

● Be sure to set out trash cans with plastic liners around your event area.

GAMES! FOOD! PRIZES! FUN! CRAFTS!

Kids and parents are invited to come for a great time at our

_____

When: _____

From: _____ To: _____

Where: _____

There'll be FUN galore— and a whole lot MORE! Hope to see you!

LEADER LEDGER

Initial planning meeting on _____.

Carnival theme: _____

Location and date: _____

Time: _____ To: _____

	Helper:	Phone:	In charge of:
1.	_____	_____	_____
2.	_____	_____	_____
3.	_____	_____	_____
4.	_____	_____	_____
5.	_____	_____	_____
6.	_____	_____	_____
7.	_____	_____	_____
8.	_____	_____	_____
9.	_____	_____	_____
10.	_____	_____	_____
11.	_____	_____	_____
12.	_____	_____	_____

CARNIVAL COUNTDOWN

Leaders: Check off each item as it's completed.

Six Weeks to Go:

❏ Recruit adult and teenage helpers and invite them to the initial planning meeting.

❏ Hold the initial planning meeting. Pray together and ask for God's guidance and help as you plan your outreach. Assign each helper or pair of helpers an activity booth. Hand out the Helper's Checklist forms and activity pages from the carnival you've chosen. Make sure all the helpers understand exactly what they're responsible for.

❏ Consider scheduling a "Carnival Capers Work Day" when you'll gather supplies, helpers, and elbow grease in one place and assemble booths together!

Five Weeks to Go:

❏ Touch base with your helpers. Be sure they're collecting the items they need to assemble their booths.

❏ If your carnival will be very large, place bulk orders for prizes, balloons, or other supplies from mail-order companies.

❏ Prepare posters and fliers for your special event.

One Month to Go:

❏ Be sure helpers are finishing their booths and have collected any prizes they're going to offer.

❏ Check in with teenagers who've signed up to help. Make sure they're still available. (Teenagers are famous for last-minute schedule changes!)

❏ Use the list on page 95 to gather the general supplies you'll need. If someone else is in charge of supplies and decorating, make sure they've made the necessary purchases.

❏ If you're planning guest entertainers such as clowns, be sure to book them for your event now.

Three Weeks to Go:

❏ Schedule a set up time just before your event. If your event will be inside, set up as early as possible. For an outside event, meet the day before to plan the arrangement of the midway.

❏ Touch base with the person in charge of general midway decorations. If you're in charge, be sure that all supplies are purchased and that you have a sketch of where you'll put each decoration.

❏ Prepare welcome cards, verse cards, or fliers you might wish to hand out with treats attached. Kids love these, and it's a great way to reinforce how much Jesus loves them!

Two Weeks to Go:

- ❑ Send or personally deliver your prepared media release to newspapers and radio stations.
- ❑ Contact a teenage helper to be in charge of the sign-in sheet. (This list of names and addresses will be an invaluable tool for follow-up contacts!)
- ❑ Photocopy the Welcome to Our Church! form on page 97. Plan to have the fliers available at the sign-in table.
- ❑ Touch base with your helpers to offer encouragement and any last minute help they may need. Be sure all booth preparations are complete.

One Week to Go:

- ❑ Touch base with the food booth helper, and be sure all food items are purchased and prepared. Be sure the helper has made a catchy price board if you plan on selling treats to defray carnival costs.
- ❑ Post fliers and posters around town, inviting people to your event.
- ❑ Call your helpers, and remind them of the meeting this week to plan your midway set up.
- ❑ Be sure you have these essentials ready: trash cans with plastic liners, signs pointing the way to restrooms, and first-aid kits.

Three Days to Go:

- ❑ Hold a last-minute organizational meeting with your helpers and volunteer teenagers. Plan where each booth will go and when its set up will occur. Be sure teenagers know what they're expected to do.
- ❑ Pray for the children and parents who will be attending your event.

One Day to Go:

- ❑ Set up your midway, and be sure decorations are up. Post restroom signs and set trash cans around the area.
- ❑ Touch base with the food booth helper to make sure all edibles are ready!
- ❑ Gather your carnival crew, and pray for your event and the children you'll reach.

Five Hours to Go:

- ❑ Finish any last minute set up. Be sure all helpers are ready.
- ❑ Check to make sure you have plenty of film and two or three cameras.
- ❑ Pray for your event, your helpers, and the children and their parents.
- ❑ Smile, and have a great time! The details will take care of themselves—God is smiling!

HELPER'S
CHECKLIST

Attach this checklist to the photocopy of your activity.

Booth or activity: _____

Materials needed for assembly:

❑ _____   ❑ _____

❑ _____   ❑ _____

❑ _____   ❑ _____

❑ _____   ❑ _____

❑ _____   ❑ _____

❑ _____   ❑ _____

❑ _____   ❑ _____

Sign for booth: _____

Prizes for booth: _____

Must be completed by: _____

GENERAL SUPPLIES

Carnival or Special Event: _____

Date of event: _____

Paper goods

- ❑ Poster board
- ❑ Paper towels
- ❑ Plastic trash bags
- ❑ _____

- ❑ _____
- ❑ _____
- ❑ _____
- ❑ _____

Decorations

- ❑ Crepe paper
- ❑ Construction paper
- ❑ _____
- ❑ _____
- ❑ _____

- ❑ Balloons
- ❑ Christmas tree lights
- ❑ _____
- ❑ _____
- ❑ _____

Prizes and "freebies"

- ❑ _____
- ❑ _____
- ❑ _____

- ❑ _____
- ❑ _____
- ❑ _____

Miscellaneous

- ❑ _____
- ❑ _____
- ❑ _____

- ❑ _____
- ❑ _____
- ❑ _____

REIMBURSEMENT FORM

Use this form to keep track of your expenses.
Staple receipts to the upper right-hand corner of this form.

Date	Cost	Description
_____	_____	_____
_____	_____	_____
_____	_____	_____
_____	_____	_____
_____	_____	_____
_____	_____	_____
_____	_____	_____
_____	_____	_____
_____	_____	_____
_____	_____	_____
_____	_____	_____

- -

MEDIA RELEASE

FOR IMMEDIATE RELEASE

CONTACT: _____

Phone: _____

_____ Church will host a community event
entitled _____. This special event will be
held on _____ from _____ to _____.
There will be prizes, games, food, and fun for all ages! The public is
invited to attend.

WELCOME TO OUR CHURCH!

We want to extend a warm welcome to you from our church family! We'd like to get to know you and want you to know us. Here is a list of our worship times and special programs.

Worship services: _____

Sunday school: _____

Children's church: _____

Evening Bible study: _____

Other: _____

Pastor: _____ Phone: _____

We'd like to extend an invitation for you
to be a part of our family!

Church name and address:

_____

_____

WELCOME ROSTER

Please sign our visitor's list so that we might welcome you to our church.

Visitor's Name: **Address & Phone:**

_____   _____

_____   _____

_____   _____

_____   _____

_____   _____

_____   _____

_____   _____

_____   _____

_____   _____

_____   _____

_____   _____

_____   _____

It was so much fun meeting you at our_____

_____!

We'd like to invite you to worship with us this Sunday.
Jesus loves you—and so do we!

_____

_____

- -

WELCOME!

Name: _____

Phone:_____

Address: _____

☐ Check here if you'd like to know more about our church.

The Great Cookie Carnival

This spur-of-the-moment celebration is short but oh-so-sweet and is a great carnival to use as a Christ-centered alternative to Halloween!

EVENT PREPARATIONS

Preparation Time
One week

Announcing the Event
Photocopy the flier on page 108. Fill in your event information, then run off photocopies to distribute around town. Enlarge the pattern to use as posters, add color, then hang them in your church and at local businesses.

General Decorations
● Hang brightly colored crepe paper streamers around your carnival midway.

● Cut circle "cookies" from construction paper. Use markers to draw chocolate chips and other decorations on the cookie cutouts. Hang the cookie cutouts around your carnival area.

● If you're celebrating outside, hang cookie cutouts, wooden spoons, and spatulas on trees and bushes. Add twinkling Christmas tree lights for a festive touch.

● Consider asking someone to dress like a chef in a large apron and paper chef's hat. (A chef's hat can also be fashioned from a white bakery sack.) Have your "chef" hand out boxes of animal crackers with notes that say, "Be a smart cookie—follow Jesus!"

FOLLOW-UP

Send a note to each guest thanking him or her for coming to your event. Consider adding recipe cards on which you've written this "recipe" for Jesus' love: "Mix 1 gallon of watchful care, 5 tons of forgiveness, 3 bushels of grace, and what do you have? Jesus' LOVE for you!"

CHOCOLATE CHIP TOSS

Try your skill with this sweet game!

Simple Supplies

You'll need a large cardboard box, gift wrap, white poster board, yellow poster board, markers, scissors, glue, tape, and three brown beanbags.

Prize Suggestions

Chocolate candy kisses

Easy Assembly

1. Cut off or fold in one set of end flaps of a large box. Cover the box with colorful gift wrap. Set the box so that its open side is facing up. You may wish to place the box on a table. If so, cover the table with bright paper.

2. Draw three large cookies on the white poster board.

3. Securely glue then tape the white poster board to one side of the box. When the glue is dry, cut a large hole in the center of each cookie shape, making sure to cut through the box, too. Be sure the holes are large enough for beanbags to pass through.

4. Make beanbags by pouring dried beans in three brown socks, then knotting the ankles. Cut off excess fabric.

5. Make a sign using the yellow poster board that says, "You're right on TARGET with JESUS!" Tape the sign on or near your booth. (You'll also need to tape a line four feet away from the "cookie box" during setup.)

At the Carnival

Let kids toss the three beanbags and try to get them through the holes in the cookies. Score a candy kiss for each bull's eye. Let kids try until they make at least one bull's eye. (Let young children and toddlers stand nearer the box.)

COOKIE STROLL

This musical game of chance is the
smart cookie's answer to a cakewalk!

Simple Supplies

You'll need four to six dozen medium-sized decorated cookies, a small table, two sheets of poster board, duct tape, scissors, ribbon, glitter glue, markers, a bowl, and index cards. You'll also need a cassette tape or CD of lively music and a cassette or CD player. (If you expect a very large turnout, make more decorated cookies. Use packaged sugar cookies to speed preparation, then frost with canned icing and add candy sprinkles.)

Prize Suggestions

Decorated cookies

Easy Assembly

1. Cut six large poster board "footsteps." Number them one to six. During setup, you'll tape the footsteps on the ground in a large circle. You may wish to cover the footsteps with clear self-adhesive paper for added durability—or cut out an extra set of footsteps in case the first set wears out.

2. Number six index cards one to six to match the footsteps. Place the cards in a bowl.

3. Decorate a small table, TV tray, or box. Set the cookies, boom box, and bowl of numbered cards on the table. (Unless your boom box has fresh batteries, you'll need to set up near an electrical outlet or have a long power cord on hand.)

4. Create a large colorful sign for your activity. Write: "Be A Smart Cookie! Follow in JESUS' footsteps!" on the sign. Embellish the letters with glitter glue. Add ribbon streamers at the corners of your sign.

At the Carnival

1. Be sure the poster board footsteps are taped in a large circle on the ground.

2. Display a plate of yummy-looking cookies, then invite six kids to stand on the footsteps.

3. Play lively music as kids march from footstep to footstep. Have kids "freeze" when you stop the music.

4. Draw a number card. The child standing on that number wins his or her choice of a decorated cookie. Continue playing with five kids, and play until only one is left. Be sure each child wins a cookie!

COOKIE RACERS

Get your engines revved for Jesus with this kooky cookie game of chance!

Simple Supplies

You'll need two sheets of poster board, a medium-sized box stuffed with newspapers, markers, drinking straws, scissors, tape, a plastic whistle, and chocolate and vanilla sandwich cookies. Plan to set up this booth on a long table.

Prize Suggestions

Small plastic cars, whistles, key chains, or cookie cutters

Easy Assembly

1. Cut two 1-inch strips the length of a sheet of poster board. These will be side rails. From the remaining portion of the poster board, cut four 3-inch squares from the top or bottom edge. You'll use the remaining length of the poster board as a racetrack. Draw and label a "Starting Line" and a "Finish Line" on either end of the racetrack. Then draw a line down the center of the racetrack to make two lanes. Tape the Starting Line end to the top of the box, slope the racetrack down, and tape the Finish Line end to the table. Tape the side rails along the edges of the racetrack.

2. Color a black and white checkerboard pattern on each of the 3-inch squares. Tape each square to a drinking straw cut in half. Attach the checkered flags at the four corners of the racetrack.

3. Use the second sheet of poster board to make a sign that says, "WIN THE RACE WITH JESUS." Hang the sign on or near your booth.

4. The sandwich cookies will serve as "race cars." Save the whistle to use during the carnival to signal the start of each race.

At the Carnival

1. Have kids line up to race two at a time. Give one child a vanilla sandwich cookie and the other child a chocolate one. Have kids place their cookies at the Starting Line and hold them vertically so they'll roll like wheels.

2. Blow your whistle to start the race. Have players let their cookies roll down the racetrack. The player whose cookie crosses the "Finish Line" first wins a prize. Let the runner-up race against a new opponent. Be sure everyone eventually gets a prize.

SMART COOKIE BAKE-OFF

Kids will love this crazy game of cookie construction.

Simple Supplies

You'll need two sheets of poster board, a brightly colored paper tablecloth, markers, a paper fastener, scissors, brown construction paper, tape, clear self-adhesive paper, and photocopies of the Cookie and Arrow patterns on page 109. You'll also need four spoons and bowls of raisins, peanuts, candy sprinkles, and chocolate chips.

Prize Suggestions

Plastic spatulas, small wooden spoons, cookie cutters, wrapped cookies, or boxes of raisins

Easy Assembly

1. Cover a table with a bright paper tablecloth.

2. Draw a game board on one sheet of poster board using the illustration at right as a guide. Color the game board with bright markers. Make a small X-cut in the center of the circle.

3. Photocopy the Cookie and Arrow patterns on page 109 onto brown construction paper. You'll need four copies of the Cookie pattern and one copy of the Arrow pattern. Cut out the cookies, and cover them with clear self-adhesive paper. Cut out the arrow, and make an X-cut near the base of the shaft. Align the arrow's X-cut with the X-cut on the game board, insert a paper fastener from front to back, and fasten it. Make sure the arrow spins freely when it's flicked.

4. Use the second sheet of poster board to make an eye-catching sign that says, "JESUS is the best ingredient in life!" Write the message in bright block letters.

5. At set-up time, attach the sign to the front of the table. Set the paper cookies, game board, and bowls of raisins, peanuts, candy sprinkles, and chocolate chips on the table. Put a spoon in each bowl.

At the Carnival

1. Invite up to four kids to play at one time. Hand each child a paper cookie.

Let one of the kids spin the arrow. If the arrow lands on an ingredient, that child may place a spoonful of that ingredient on his or her paper cookie. Then let the other children take turns. The first child to get all four ingredients wins a prize. If the spinner lands on an ingredient the child already has, skip to the next player. If the spinner lands on the word "Jesus," the game is over and everyone wins a prize.

2. Play until all the kids complete their cookies or until the spinner lands on the word "Jesus." Have kids return the ingredients to the correct bowls, and be sure everyone gets a prize.

COOKIE CRAFT BOOTH

Invite kids to "make a memory" at this exciting craft booth!

Simple Supplies

For the first craft you'll need poster board, a brightly colored paper tablecloth, ribbon, cookie cutters, tape, markers, small cookies, a hot glue gun, and bar pins. For the second craft, you'll need packaged sugar cookies, plastic knives, canned icing, small bowls, food coloring, napkins, and candy sprinkles.

Easy Assembly

1. Cover a table with a bright paper tablecloth. Hang cookie cutters from the edge of the table with ribbon. Plan to place this booth near an electrical outlet.

2. Use poster board and markers to create a sign that says, "Create-a-Craft!"

3. Use one half of the table for making cookie pins. Set out small cookies, markers, bar pins, and a hot glue gun. *Keep the hot glue gun under the table where guests cannot reach it.*

4. Use the other half of the table for creative cookie decorating. Set out candy sprinkles, plastic knives, napkins, packaged sugar cookies, and small bowls of canned icing tinted with food coloring.

At the Carnival

1. To make cookie pins, let kids use colored markers to write "Jesus" or draw a cross on small cookies. Have an adult or a teenage helper hot glue bar pins to the decorated cookies. Let kids wear their pins home.

2. At the cookie decorating side of the table, let kids use their choice of colored icings and decorations to design their own "dream cookies," then take their creations home to show off or munch!

TREATS TO EAT 'N' SELL

Munch delightful treats at the carnival— or take them home to enjoy later.

> Cookie Lollys _____ 50¢
>
> Personalized Brownies _____ 50¢
>
> Apple Juice _____ 35¢

Simple Supplies

You'll need poster board, brightly colored paper or fabric, scissors, markers, plastic sandwich bags, plastic knives, craft sticks, ribbon, canned icing, packaged chocolate chip cookies, prepared brownies, tube icing, paper cups, napkins, and apple juice.

Easy Assembly

1. Cover a table with bright paper or fabric. Use poster board and bright markers to create a price board. Use the illustration above as a guide.

2. Prepare Cookie Lollys by spreading icing between two chocolate chip cookies, then inserting a craft stick between them. Cover the cookie portion with a plastic sandwich bag, then use ribbon to gather and tie the bag. Suggested price: 50 cents.

3. Set out plain brownies. When a guest purchases a brownie, use tube icing to write the guest's initials in fancy letters. Slide the decorated brownies into plastic sandwich bags or serve on napkins. Suggested price: 50 cents.

4. Serve cups of chilled apple juice for a refreshing beverage. Suggested price: 35 cents.

COME TO THE GREAT

COOKIE CARNIVAL!

Games, Prizes, Food, and Fun for All!

Where: _____

Date: _____

Time: _____

Kids, bring your parents and friends!

Spinner Arrow

Ark-in-the-Park Carnival

The Theme

Noah and the ark

Spend an exciting time with Noah and his family as kids pet real animals and enjoy a "zooful" of great games and activities!

EVENT PREPARATIONS

Preparation Time
One month

Announcing the Event
Photocopy the flier on page 118. Post fliers in grocery stores, veterinarians' offices, pet stores, and the local library. Enlarge the flier and add color to create posters. If you're hanging invitations on doorknobs around the neighborhood, photocopy the Free Coupon pattern on page 119, and attach it to each flier. Be sure to order plenty of small, animal-shaped erasers if you're handing out the coupons.

General Decorations
● Gather a few volunteers to construct an ark. If you have access to playground climbing equipment, simply use duct tape to cover the sides with large pieces of cardboard. Or put together a long, wooden rectangle, then cover it with paneling or leave it as is and explain that Noah is in the process of building the ark! This carnival is best suited for outdoors, but if you're inside, create an ark from tables pushed together or appliance boxes duct taped together.

● If you're holding this event outside, put up a small rolled-wire fence to hold a petting zoo. Contact local farmers to bring lambs or goats for petting—or ask someone with puppies or rabbits to consider bringing them.

● Enlarge the Animal patterns on page 44. Color the patterns, then mount them on poster board. Display pairs of these animals around the midway. Tack the Monkey patterns onto tree trunks or hang them from tree branches. Fasten the Parrot patterns in bushes and trees!

● Ask volunteers to dress up as members of Noah's family. Use bathrobes, sandals, towels or scarves to cover their heads, and colorful neckties as belts and headbands. Let "Noah" carry a tool belt or hammer and a set of blueprints! Have

"Mrs. Noah" hand out animal crackers and small cards with Scripture verses on them. Post two or three members of "Noah's family" by the ark, and encourage them to tell the story of Noah to your young guests.

● If there's someone in your congregation who knows how to twist balloons into animal shapes, enlist his or her help and provide bulk quantities of balloons. Be sure to create a balloon animal for each child to take home.

FOLLOW-UP

Send each guest a thank you note. Sending a small animal-shaped eraser along with the note is a nice way to reinforce the good feelings your guests had at the event—and may spur them on to consider joining you for worship!

CATCH-A-CRITTER

Invite kids to go fishing for animal pairs.

Simple Supplies

You'll need a ½-inch-diameter dowel, fishing line, paper clips, a magnet, poster board, scissors, blue paper tablecloth, blue crepe paper, tape, markers, masking tape, a table, a shoe box or basket, glue, clear self-adhesive paper, and photocopies of the Animals patterns on page 44.

Prize suggestions

Small animal figurines, boxes of animal crackers, toothbrushes, combs, balloons, or colorful shoelaces

Easy Assembly

1. Photocopy the Animal patterns on page 44 onto stiff paper. Be sure you have two of every kind of animal. Color the animals, then cover them with clear self-adhesive paper. Cut out the animal pairs, and attach a paper clip to each animal.

2. Tie a 3-foot length of fishing line to the end of the dowel. Wrap a bit of tape around the fishing line to secure it to the "fishing pole." Tie the magnet on the other end of the fishing line to create a "hook."

3. Cover the front and sides of a table with a blue paper tablecloth. Twist blue crepe paper, and tape it to the edges of the table to make "waves." You may wish to tape pictures of colorful fish cut from fish-print gift wrap to the front of the table. During setup, place a masking tape line three feet from the table.

4. Make a colorful poster board sign that says, "God Brought the Animals Two by Two" Glue or tape extra paper animals to the sign. You may want to outline the letters and animals with glitter glue.

At the Carnival

1. Scatter one set of paper animals with paper clips on the booth table. Place the rest of the animals in a shoe box or basket.

2. Invite each child to draw a paper animal from the shoe box or basket. Then hand the child the fishing pole, and invite him or her to "fish" for the animal that matches the one drawn from the box. If the child "hooks" the matching animal, let him or her choose a prize. Let kids who hook a nonmatching animal keep trying until they catch the matching animal. Be sure everyone gets a prize!

AWESOME ANIMALS FACE PAINTING

Turn your guests into cuddly—or "ferocious"—animals with this fun activity booth.

Simple Supplies

You'll need acrylic craft paint, paintbrushes, bowls of water, a table, paper towels, construction paper, tape, scissors, orange poster board, markers, and orange and black crepe paper and balloons.

Prize suggestions

None needed

Easy Assembly

1. Cut paper ears and tails from construction paper. Cut out black and orange pointed tiger or cat ears; long, pink bunny ears; black and orange tails; and puffy, white bunny tails. For extra fun, add stripes to the orange tails and cotton balls to the bunny tails.

2. Use the poster board to create an exciting sign that says, "AWESOME ANIMALS FACE PAINTING" in tiger-striped letters. Tape the sign to the front of a table.

3. Twist the orange and black crepe paper, then tape the paper along the edges of a table. Tape a few crepe paper streamers at the corners of your sign. Add a few orange and black balloons to complete your preparation.

4. The day of the carnival, set out acrylic craft paint, paintbrushes, water, paper towels, tape, and the paper ears and tails.

At the Carnival

1. Be sure you're wearing your best "animal face," paper ears, and tail to show kids how much fun it is to pretend! Invite your young guests to turn into cats, tigers, bunnies, or imaginary animals by choosing ears and tails, then having their faces painted. Tape the paper ears and tails in place.

2. For a neat touch, have an instant-print camera ready to take your animal friends' pictures when they're all "duded up"! Let guests take their photos home as souvenirs.

LEAPIN' FROGS!

Kids will love this funny game of chance!

When God said "GO," Noah **HOPPED** to it!

Simple Supplies

You'll need green poster board, yellow poster board, balloons, glue, tape, a permanent black marker, markers, scissors, a 6-inch by 2-foot wooden plank, a brick, masking tape, a wooden meat mallet, dried beans, and a pair of green socks.

Prize Suggestions

Plastic toy bugs, small toy frogs, or green lollipops

Easy Assembly

1. Make a pair of beanbag frogs by pouring dried beans into green socks, then knotting the ankles securely. Cut off the excess fabric. Use a permanent black marker to add googly eyes and big grins.

2. Cut several oval lily pads about 1 foot in length from green poster board. Cut flowers from part of the yellow poster board, then glue the flowers onto the lily pads.

3. Use the remaining yellow poster board to make a sunny sign that says, "When God Said 'GO,' Noah HOPPED to it!" Add small green and yellow lily pads around the edge of the sign for a festive touch. Tape balloons to the corners of the sign.

4. During setup, place the lily pads on the ground in an area about 3 feet square. Place a brick about four feet from the lily pads, then balance a wooden plank on the brick. Set a beanbag frog on one end of the plank. Now test your game. Catapult a beanbag frog to the lily pads by hitting the other end of the plank with a meat mallet. If the beanbag frog doesn't reach the lily pads, adjust the distance of either the lily pads or the catapult. (You may wish to have kids use their fists or feet instead of a meat mallet.)

At the Carnival

Demonstrate how to catapult the beanbag frogs to the lily pads, then invite kids to try. Give a prize when any part of a frog lands on a lily pad. Let each child try until he or she lands a frog. Be sure everyone gets a prize.

FEED THE ELEPHANTS

Kids will love tossing peanuts through an elephant's mouth to win a prize!

Simple Supplies

You'll need four sheets of gray poster board, one sheet of poster board of any color, scissors, two "crinkly" hoses from vacuum cleaners, duct tape, a medium-sized box, jungle-print gift wrap, tape, construction paper, peanuts in the shell, and four ½-inch-diameter dowels or two boxes.

Prize Suggestions

Bags of peanuts, small toy elephants, or candy peanuts

Easy Assembly

1. Use gray poster board to create two large elephant heads using the illustration at right as a guide. Cut an open mouth on each elephant. Add construction paper eyes and tusks. To make trunks, attach vacuum cleaner hoses

with duct tape. Tape the trunks up as if the elephants are trumpeting.

2. Use duct tape to fasten a dowel vertically to either side of an elephant head for stability. During setup, you'll push the dowels into the ground to serve as stakes. If your event will be indoors, stabilize the elephant heads by using two boxes that each have one set of end flaps open, then tape each elephant head to the outspread flaps.

3. Cover the medium-sized box with jungle-print gift wrap. Use a sheet of poster board and cut construction paper letters to create a colorful sign that says, "FEED NOAH'S ELEPHANTS." Glue peanuts in the shell around the sign, and attach it to the front of the box.

4. During setup, place a 3-foot duct tape "tossing line" five feet from the elephant heads. Have ready a bag of peanuts in the shell.

At the Carnival

Invite kids to stand at the tossing line and toss peanuts into the elephants' mouths. When a child feeds both elephants, have him or her choose a prize. Let kids play until they each win a prize. You may want to let younger children stand closer to the elephants.

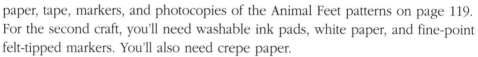

CREATIVE CRAFTS BOOTH

Invite kids to have a roarin' good time creating make-to-take crafts.

Simple Supplies

For the first craft, you'll need white shelf paper, a long table, balloons, poster board, construction paper, tape, markers, and photocopies of the Animal Feet patterns on page 119. For the second craft, you'll need washable ink pads, white paper, and fine-point felt-tipped markers. You'll also need crepe paper.

Easy Assembly

1. Before carnival time, photocopy and cut out the Animal Feet patterns on page 119. Use these paper cutouts as guides to cut poster board feet patterns for kids to trace. Be sure to have two of each pattern ready. Cut a 6-inch poster board square for each guest.

2. Cover a long table with white shelf paper and tape it in place. On one-half of the table, set out balloons, markers, construction paper, tape, the poster board animal feet patterns, and poster board squares.

3. On the other half of the table, set out ink pads, paper, and fine-tipped markers.

4. Use poster board and glitter glue to create an inviting sign that says, "Creative Crafts." Add crepe paper streamers and balloons to the sign for a festive touch.

At the Carnival

1. To make balloon animals, help kids blow up and tie balloons. Then have kids trace the poster board feet patterns onto the poster board squares, cut out the feet, and cut the slits. When kids slide the balloons' knotted ends into the slits, the balloons will stand upright. Let kids tape construction paper ears, feathers, eyes, beaks, whiskers, or stripes onto their balloons to make realistic or crazy animals. Caution kids not to remove the tape once it's attached to the balloons!

2. To make thumbprint animals, hand each child a sheet of white paper. Have each child press one thumb onto an ink pad then stamp his or her thumbprint on the paper. Encourage kids to add features with fine-tipped markers.

TREATS TO EAT 'N' SELL

Make these tummy-tickling treats to eat and sell!

Treats to Eat

Edible Ark Dough..... 50¢

Animals on the Ark Cookies............ 50¢

Juice................ 50¢

Simple Supplies

You'll need brightly colored paper or fabric, a table, poster board, markers, plastic sandwich bags, powdered sugar, peanut butter, twist ties, ribbon, scissors, pineapple-orange juice, paper cups, napkins, packaged sugar cookies, canned icing, rainbow candy sprinkles, and animal crackers.

Easy Assembly

1. Cover a table with bright paper or fabric. Use poster board and bright markers to create a price board. Use the illustration above as a guide.

2. Prepare Edible Ark Dough by mixing one part peanut butter and two parts powdered sugar. If the dough is too sticky, add more powdered sugar. Place a golf ball-sized lump of dough in a plastic sandwich bag, then seal the bag with a twist-tie wire. Tie a ribbon around the bag. If the day is very warm, you may wish to keep the dough chilled in an ice chest. Suggested price: 50 cents.

3. Prepare Animals on the Ark cookies by icing packaged sugar cookies, then sprinkling them with rainbow candy sprinkles. Add an animal cracker to the top of each cookie. Slide cookies into plastic sandwich bags, then tie the bags with ribbon. Suggested price: 50 cents.

4. Serve chilled pineapple-orange juice in paper cups. Suggested price: 50 cents.

COME TWO BY TWO! COME ONE, COME ALL, TO THE

ARK·IN·THE·PARK CARNIVAL!

Where:_____

Date: _____

Time: _____

Games! Prizes! Food! And Fun for All!

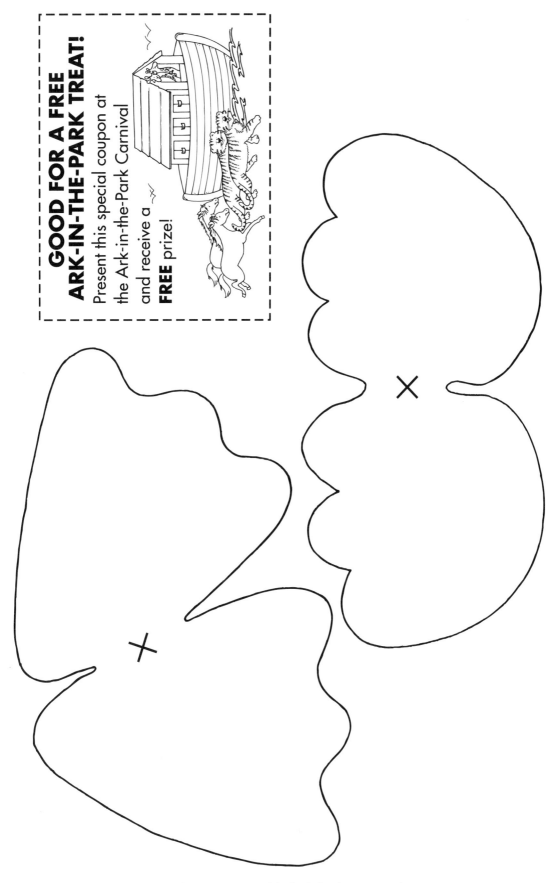

Special Event in Bethlehem

Take a joyous step back in time and treat your young guests to a visit to Bethlehem.

The Theme
Christmas

EVENT PREPARATIONS

Preparation Time
One month

Announcing the Event

Photocopy the flier on page 129. Place the flier at local businesses and holiday bazaars. If you plan to hang fliers on doorknobs, you may wish to attach small candy canes. Create a poster for the front of your church by enlarging the flier and adding color.

General Decorations

● No Christmas event is complete without a Nativity scene—and a living Nativity is the most memorable! Make a stable from plywood or large appliance boxes. Place bundles of straw on the roof to give the appearance of thatch, and scatter loose straw on the stable floor. Attach an electric Christmas star ornament to the top of the stable. A few live sheep add a wonderful touch, but sheep figures cut from plywood or cardboard are easier to clean up after! Place a wrapped baby doll in a manger made from a small wooden or cardboard box. Ask two teenagers or older children to play the parts of Mary and Joseph.

● Make palm trees to accent your event area by twisting brown paper grocery sacks into long, thin trunks, then taping them to walls or to real trees with duct tape. Enlarge and photocopy onto green construction paper the Tropical Leaf pattern on page 44. Cut out the leaves and fringe the edges to make palm fronds. Use duct tape to attach the fronds to the paper trunks.

● Hang glittery poster board stars from the ceiling. Put up strands of tiny white or gold Christmas tree lights around your celebration area to add a festive touch.

● Ask helpers and volunteers to dress up as people in Bethlehem might have dressed at the time of Jesus' birth. Simple costumes can be made from bathrobes tied with rope belts, sandals, and towels with bright necktie headbands for headdresses.

● Cut brown and gray construction paper "cobblestones" for the floor.

Follow-Up

Send special notes decorated with self-adhesive star stickers to the kids who attended your event. Thank them for sharing a wonderful time, and invite them to bring their families to church to worship with you.

NO ROOM!

Meet Bethlehem's famous innkeeper and play a fun game of chance.

Simple Supplies

You'll need construction paper, markers, straw or shredded paper, brown paper grocery sacks, glue, brown or yellow poster board, tape, scissors, index cards, a large basket, five large boxes, a cassette or CD player, and cassette or CD of Christmas music.

Prize Suggestions

Shiny keys, key chains that read "Bethlehem Inn," combs, or toothbrushes

Easy Assembly

1. Make Bible time "inns" by covering five large boxes with brown paper cut from grocery sacks. Glue straw or shredded paper to the rooftops. Add doors and windows cut from construction paper. Use a marker to number the inns one to five.

2. Create a rustic-looking sign with brown poster board that says, "Any Room at the Inn?" Add wood-grain effects with a black marker.

3. Write the numbers one to five on separate index cards and place the cards in a large basket.

4. During setup, arrange the "inns of Bethlehem" in a medium-sized circle. Be sure to position the game near an electrical outlet for the cassette or CD player.

At the Carnival

1. Dress up as the innkeeper, and tell bits and pieces of the Christmas story to the children, focusing on Mary and Joseph's arrival in Bethlehem and how there was no room for them to stay in.

2. Invite five children to play each round of the game. Have kids stand in a circle around the inns. Explain that as the music plays, they can walk in a circle, tapping each inn as they pass. When the music stops, have kids stand by the inns nearest them. Draw a number card from the basket. The player who is standing by the inn with the matching number receives a prize and is then out of the game. Ask another child to fill his or her place and continue playing. Play until each child has won a prize.

CAMEL BOWLING

Kids will love this goofy game of skill!

Simple Supplies

You'll need poster board, three empty half-gallon milk cartons, markers, brown paper grocery sacks, construction paper, plastic jewels, tape, photocopies of the Camel pattern on page 131, masking tape, a basket, glue, a large box or small table, crepe paper, scissors, three tennis balls, and twine.

Prize Suggestions

Boxes of animal crackers, small animal-shaped erasers, plastic "jewels," or note pads

Easy Assembly

1. Cover the milk cartons with brown paper cut from grocery sacks. Make four photocopies of the Camel pattern on page 131 onto brown construction paper, then cut them out. Glue a paper camel cutout to the front of each milk carton. Cut 5-inch pieces of twine, and glue them to the camel cutouts for tails.

2. Cover a large box or a small table with brown paper cut from grocery sacks. Twist, then tape crepe paper along the edges of the box, and cut crepe paper streamers for the corners. Place the tennis balls and the basket of prizes on top of the box.

3. Make a catchy poster board sign that says, "CAMEL BOWLING." Glue the remaining camel cutout on the sign, then attach the sign to the front of the box.

4. During setup, place the booth in front of a wall or corner. Place a 3-foot masking tape line on the floor or ground beside your box. Stand the three camels 15 feet from the tape line. (You may wish to position the camels in front of a wall or where two walls intersect.)

5. Plan to dress up like one of the wise men. Use a fancy bathrobe with a colorful necktie belt. Make a poster board crown and glue on plastic jewels.

At the Carnival

1. Chat with kids about the wise men. Explain that they traveled a long distance on camels to find Jesus so they could worship him and give him fine gifts.

2. Let kids take turns bowling over the camels. Hand each child three tennis balls, and have them stand behind the line and roll the balls at the camels. If a player knocks over a camel, he or she gets to choose a gift. Be sure everyone wins a gift. (You may want to let younger children stand a bit closer to the camels.)

SHEEP RACES

Happy young shepherds will have a silly time racing their pretend sheep.

Simple Supplies

You'll need four white plastic trash bags, newspaper, black construction paper, a black permanent marker, tape, twist ties, masking tape, two ½-inch-diameter dowels, and balloons.

Prize Suggestions

Baby food jars filled with cotton balls, bags of cotton candy, or candy cane "staffs"

Easy Assembly

1. Stuff four white plastic trash bags with newspaper to make fluffy "sheep." Secure the ends of the bags with twist-tie wires to create sheep's "tails." Add black construction paper ears and noses to the sheep. Use a black permanent marker to add eyes and smiles.

2. During setup, place two masking tape lines 20 feet apart. Between the two lines, set up an obstacle course by taping five or six balloons to the ground. Set the sheep and the two dowel "staffs" next to one of the lines.

3. Plan to dress up as a shepherd. Carry a cane or large stick for a staff and wear sandals and a bathrobe tied with a rope.

At the Carnival

1. Chat with children about the shepherds in the fields and how angels told them the good news about Jesus' birth.

2. Invite pairs of children to race. Give each child a staff and two sheep. Have the racers use their staffs to move their two sheep back and forth around the balloons to the other line, then back to the first line. Explain that no hands are allowed—only staffs may be used to guide the sheep. Let the child who finishes first choose a prize, then let the runner-up choose a prize, too.

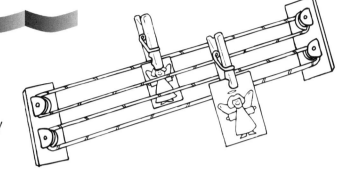

ANGEL FLIGHT

Help angels "fly" with the good news about Jesus' birth!

Simple Supplies

You'll need four pulley wheels, screws and a screwdriver, two 8×10-inch scraps of wood, photocopies of the Angel pattern on page 130, 20 feet of clothesline rope, duct tape, scissors, self-adhesive bows, poster board, markers, two hinge-style clothespins, glitter glue, a large box, gift wrap, and two yardsticks.

Prize Suggestions

Small angel figurines, angel bookmarks, toy megaphones, or note pads and pencils

Easy Assembly

1. Attach two pulley wheels to each 8×10-inch piece of wood. Be sure the pulley wheels are parallel to each other on the boards. String the clothesline rope over the pulleys. During setup, attach the pulley boards to walls or trees or attach them to two sturdy chairs using utility clamps. Be sure the rope is taut and can be easily pulled back and forth over both sets of pulleys.

2. Photocopy the Angel pattern on page 130 onto stiff paper. Color and cut out two angels. During setup, attach each angel cutout to the rope with a clothespin.

3. Make a booth by covering the front and sides of a large box with gift wrap. Angel-print gift wrap adds a wonderful touch! Decorate the box with self-adhesive bows. Use duct tape to attach the yardsticks vertically on either side of the box. The yardsticks will support a sign.

4. Use poster board and markers to make a sign that says, "HAVE YOU HEARD? JESUS IS BORN!" Outline the letters with glitter glue. Tape the sign to the yardsticks on the booth.

5. Plan to dress up as an angel. Wear a white robe or sheet, sandals, and silver or gold Christmas tree garland as a halo.

At the Carnival

1. Chat with kids about how the angels announced Jesus' birth to the shepherds.

2. Use clothespins to attach the angel cutouts to the rope. Be sure the pulleys are working smoothly.

3. Invite two children at a time to "fly" the angels across the "sky." Assure the kids that this isn't a competitive race and that both angels will tell the good news about Jesus' birth.

4. When the angels reach the other end of the pulleys, have kids shout, "Jesus is born," then pull the angels back to the starting place. Then let each child choose a gift.

CHRISTMAS CRAFTS BOOTH

Invite kids to make a Christmas toy and a Christmas keepsake.

Simple Supplies

For the first craft, you'll need a long table, poster board, scissors, white shelf paper, markers, crepe paper, craft sticks, construction paper, tacky craft glue, tape, fishing line, and self-adhesive foil stars. For the second craft, you'll need drinking straws, yellow poster board, scissors, pencils, jingle bells, and tape. You'll also need purple, white, and blue ribbon.

Easy Assembly

1. Cover a long table with white shelf paper. Cut colorful crepe paper streamers, and tape them along the edges and corners of the table. Make an inviting sign from poster board that says, "Christmas Crafts" in bright letters, then tape crepe paper streamers to the top corners of the sign. Hang the sign on or by the table.

2. Cut three or four 5-inch star shapes from poster board. Also cut 5-inch lengths of different colors of ribbon. Each child will need three lengths of ribbon.

At the Carnival

1. On one-half of the table kids will make Nativity ornaments. Set out craft sticks, tacky craft glue, construction paper, self-adhesive foil stars, and fishing line. Have kids glue three craft sticks in a triangle and stick a foil star to the top of the triangle. Let kids cut or tear simple construction paper shapes for Mary, Joseph, the manger, and baby Jesus then glue the figures to the bottom craft stick. Add a fishing-line loop for a hanger.

2. On the other half of the table kids will make festive Star Stix. Set out drinking straws, pencils, jingle bells, 5-inch lengths of ribbon, scissors, yellow poster board, and tape. Have kids trace around the star shapes on yellow poster board, then cut them out. (Young children will need an older buddy to help with this step.) Help kids tape the stars to one end of a drinking straw then tape three ribbons to the bottom of the star and tie a jingle bell to one of the ribbons. (Because of choking hazard, you'll need to purchase larger, 1-inch jingle bells if very young children participate in this activity.)

TREATS TO EAT 'N' SELL

What's a Christmas celebration without festive goodies?

Festive Foods

StrawMangers ..... 50¢
King's Crown
Cookies .... 50¢
Holiday Punch ..... 50¢

Simple Supplies

You'll need brightly colored paper or fabric, poster board, markers, plastic sandwich bags, chocolate chips, wax paper, ribbon, chow mein noodles, jelly beans, packaged sugar cookies, icing, gumdrops, napkins, paper cups, and cranberry or cherry juice.

Easy Assembly

1. Cover a table with bright paper or fabric. Use poster board and bright markers to create a price board for the treats you're planning to sell. Use the illustration above as a guide.

2. Prepare Straw Mangers by melting chocolate chips in a double boiler or microwave oven. Gently stir chow mein noodles into the melted chocolate. Drop tablespoons of the mixture on wax paper. Before the treats have completely cooled, add a jelly bean "baby" to each manger. Slide one or two mangers into a plastic sandwich bag and tie it with a ribbon. Suggested price: 50 cents.

3. Prepare King's Crown Cookies by icing packaged sugar cookies. Snip gumdrops in half and add five or six gumdrop "jewels" to the top of each cookie. Slide the cookies into plastic sandwich bags and tie the bags with ribbons. Suggested price: 50 cents.

4. Serve cranberry or cherry juice for Holiday Punch. If you'd like a little festive sparkle, add lemon-lime soda to the juice. Suggested price: 50 cents.

It's a special event in Bethlehem!
Come join us for a celebration
of God's love!

Where: _____

Date: _____

Time: _____

Games! Prizes! Food! And Fun for All!

Appendix

The following manufacturers may be able to supply many of your party and special event needs for lower-than-retail prices—especially if you buy items in bulk quantities!

Party Favors and Carnival Prizes

- Oriental Trading Company
  Box 2049
  Omaha, NE 68103
  800-327-9678

- M & N International
  13860 West Laurel Drive
  Lake Forest, IL 60045
  (708) 680-4700

- U.S. Toy
  1227 East 119th Street
  Grandview, MO 64030
  800-255-6124

Paper Goods and Decorations

- Current, Inc.
  1025 East Woodman
  Colorado Springs, CO 80918
  800-525-7170

- The Party Basket, Ltd.
  734 Nashville Avenue
  New Orleans, LA 70115
  (504) 899-8126

- Beistle Company
  Box 10
  Shippensburg, PA 17257
  (717) 532-2135

Miscellaneous Supplies

Balloons

● The following are great books about creating balloon animals for decorations and party entertainment: *Balloon Animals* and *Balloon Hats & Accessories* by Aaron Hsu-Flanders. They come complete with balloons and an air pump! These books are available from:

Contemporary Books
180 North Stetson
Chicago, IL 60601
(312) 782-9181

● The "Happy Helium Balloon Kit" comes complete with 20 3-inch balloons and an aerosol can of helium to inflate them. Order the "Happy Helium Balloon Kit" from:

Edmund's Scientific
101 East Gloucester Pike
Barrington, NJ 08007-1380
(609) 573-6250

Evaluation of *Group's Party! Party! for Children's Ministry*

Please help Group Publishing, Inc., continue to provide innovative and usable resources for ministry by taking a moment to fill out and send us this evaluation. Thanks!

● ● ●

1. As a whole, this book has been (circle one):

Not much help   Very helpful

1   2   3   4   5   6   7   8   9   10

2. The things I liked best about this book were:

3. This book could be improved by:

4. One thing I'll do differently because of this book is:

5. Optional Information:

Name _____

Street Address _____

City _____ State _____ Zip _____

Phone Number _____ Date _____

BRING THE BIBLE TO LIFE FOR YOUR 1ST THROUGH 6TH GRADERS WITH GROUP'S HANDS-ON BIBLE CURRICULUM™

Energize your kids with Active Learning!

Group's **Hands-On Bible Curriculum**™ will help you teach the Bible in a radical new way. It's based on Active Learning—the same teaching method Jesus used.

In each lesson, students will participate in exciting and memorable learning experiences using fascinating gadgets and gizmos you've not seen with any other curriculum. Your elementary students will discover biblical truths and <u>remember</u> what they learn because they're <u>doing</u> instead of just listening.

You'll save time and money too!

While students are learning more, you'll be working less—simply follow the quick and easy instructions in the **Teachers Guide**. You'll get tons of material for an energy-packed 35- to 60- minute lesson. In addition to the easy-to-use **Teachers Guide**, you'll get all the essential teaching materials you need in a ready-to-use **Learning Lab**®. Plus, you'll SAVE BIG over other curriculum programs that require you to buy expensive separate student books—all student handouts in Group's **Hands-On Bible Curriculum** are photocopiable!

Challenging topics each quarter keep your kids coming back!

Group's **Hands-On Bible Curriculum** covers topics that matter to your kids and teaches them the Bible with integrity. Switching topics every month keeps your 1st- through 6th-graders enthused and coming back for more. The full two-year program will help your kids...
- make God-pleasing decisions,
- recognize their God-given potential, and
- seek to grow as Christians.

Take the boredom out of Sunday school, children's church, and youth group for your elementary students. Make your job easier and more rewarding with no-fail lessons that are ready in a flash. Order Group's **Hands-On Bible Curriculum** for your 1st- through 6th-graders today.

Hands-On Bible Curriculum is also available for Toddlers & 2s, Preschool, and Pre-K and K!

Order today from your local Christian bookstore, or write: Group Publishing, Box 485, Loveland, CO 80539.